Rick Steves

WITHDRAWN

SNAPSHOT

Edinburgh

CONTENTS

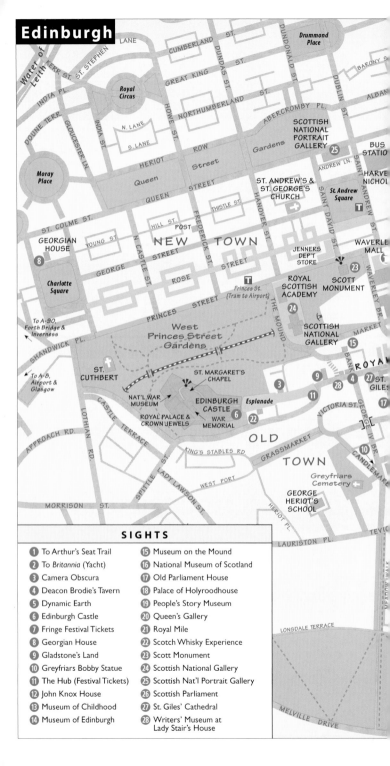

Edinburgh

SIGHTS

1. To Arthur's Seat Trail
2. To *Britannia* (Yacht)
3. Camera Obscura
4. Deacon Brodie's Tavern
5. Dynamic Earth
6. Edinburgh Castle
7. Fringe Festival Tickets
8. Georgian House
9. Gladstone's Land
10. Greyfriars Bobby Statue
11. The Hub (Festival Tickets)
12. John Knox House
13. Museum of Childhood
14. Museum of Edinburgh
15. Museum on the Mound
16. National Museum of Scotland
17. Old Parliament House
18. Palace of Holyroodhouse
19. People's Story Museum
20. Queen's Gallery
21. Royal Mile
22. Scotch Whisky Experience
23. Scott Monument
24. Scottish National Gallery
25. Scottish Nat'l Portrait Gallery
26. Scottish Parliament
27. St. Giles' Cathedral
28. Writers' Museum at Lady Stair's House

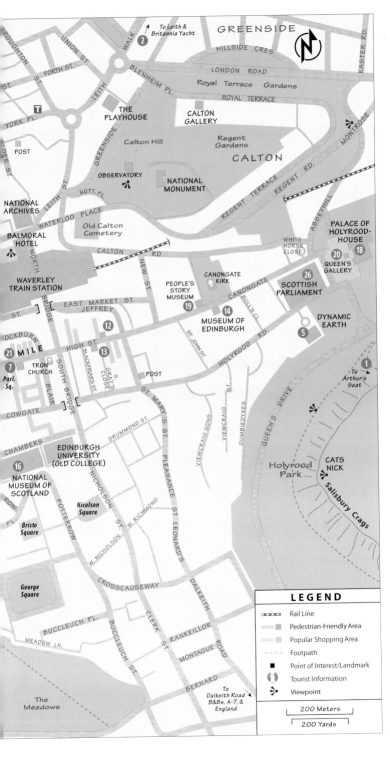

Scotland

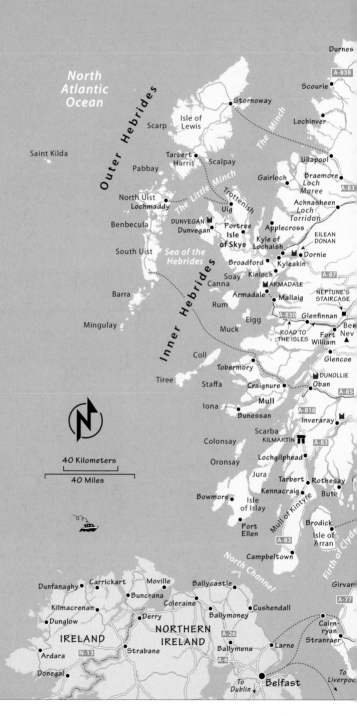

INTRODUCTION

This Snapshot guide, excerpted from my guidebook *Rick Steves Scotland*, introduces you to the rugged, feisty, colorful capital city of Edinburgh. A hubbub of innovation and tradition, this urbane city rambles along seven hills on the banks of the Firth of Forth. Its historic Royal Mile links Edinburgh Castle—home of Mary Queen of Scots—to the Palace of Holyroodhouse, the home away from home of today's Queen Elizabeth. To the north is the city's New Town, a characteristic 18th-century neighborhood of Georgian mansions and upscale hangouts.

Edinburgh is the political, cultural, and intellectual center of Scotland, but intrepid visitors can still find a few surviving rough edges of "Auld Reekie," as it was once called (for the smell of smoke during the Victorian era). Take a walk along historic cobbled streets and narrow lanes, tracing the footsteps of Robert Burns and Robert Louis Stevenson. Sip whisky with an expert and see firsthand how Scotland's national drink can become, as they're fond of saying, "a very good friend." Debate the pros and cons of Scottish independence on the steps of the 21st-century parliament building. Through it all, be prepared for a Scottish charm offensive that will make you want to stay longer in one of Europe's most intoxicating capitals.

To help you have the best trip possible, I've included the following topics in this book:

- **Planning Your Time,** with advice on how to make the most of your limited time
- **Orientation,** including tourist information (abbreviated as TI), tips on public transportation, local tour options, and helpful hints

- **Sights** with ratings:
    - ▲▲▲—Don't miss
    - ▲▲—Try hard to see
    - ▲—Worthwhile if you can make it
    - **No rating**—Worth knowing about
- **Sleeping** and **Eating,** with good-value recommendations in every price range
- **Connections,** with tips on trains, buses, and driving

Practicalities, near the end of this book, has information on money, staying connected, hotel reservations, transportation, and other helpful hints.

To travel smartly, read this little book in its entirety before you go. It's my hope that this guide will make your trip more meaningful and rewarding. Traveling like a temporary local, you'll get the absolute most out of every mile, minute, and dollar.

Happy travels!

Rick Steves

SCOTLAND

One of the three countries that make up Great Britain, rugged, feisty, colorful Scotland stands apart. Whether it's the laid-back, less-organized nature of the people, the stony architecture, the unmanicured landscape, or simply the haggis, go-its-own-way Scotland is distinctive.

Scotland encompasses about a third of Britain's geographical area (30,400 square miles), but has less than a tenth of its population (about 5.4 million). This sparsely populated chunk of land stretches to Norwegian latitudes. Its Shetland Islands, at about 60°N (similar to Anchorage, Alaska), are the northernmost point of the British Isles. You may see Scotland referred to as "Caledonia" (its ancient Roman name) or "Alba" (its Gaelic name). Scotland's fortunes were long tied to the sea; all of its leading cities are located along firths (estuaries), where major rivers connect to ocean waters.

The southern part of Scotland, called the Lowlands, is relatively flat and urbanized. The northern area—the Highlands—features a wild, severely undulating terrain, punctuated by lochs (lakes) and fringed by sea lochs (inlets) and islands.

The Highland Boundary Fault that divides Scotland geologically also divides it culturally. Historically, there were two distinct identities: rougher Highlanders in the northern wilderness and the more refined Lowlanders in the southern flat-

Scotland Almanac

Official Name: Scotland.

Population: About 5.4 million. Scotland is mostly English-speaking, though about 1.5 million people use the Scots "language," and about 60,000 speak Scottish Gaelic.

Latitude and Longitude: 57°N and 4°W. The Shetland Islands are Scotland's northernmost point, at 60°N (similar to Anchorage, Alaska).

Area: 30,400 square miles, about the size of South Carolina.

Geography: Scotland's flatter southern portion is the Lowlands; the Highlands to the north are more wild and hilly, and the country boasts over 6,000 miles of coastline and more than 790 islands (only about 130 are inhabited). Ben Nevis in western Scotland (at 4,406 feet) is Great Britain's highest peak.

Biggest Cities: Glasgow has 600,000 people, Edinburgh 490,000.

Economy: The gross domestic product is about $142 billion, and the GDP per capita is $26,500. The Scottish service sector (including retail and financial services) has become an increasingly significant part of its economy, producing over 60 percent of all economic activity in 2015.

Scotland's main exports include food and drink, as well as chemicals and petroleum products. Scotch whisky comprises a quarter of all UK food and drink exports; exports to the US represent the biggest market for Scotch by value, though France is the biggest market by volume.

Scotland uses the same currency as the other UK countries of England, Wales, and Northern Ireland: the pound sterling.

Government: Queen Elizabeth II officially heads the country—but for Scots she is simply Queen Elizabeth, not Queen Elizabeth II. (Scotland and England were separate monarchies when England had their first Elizabeth.) Theresa May is the UK's prime minister, and Nicola Sturgeon is Scotland's first minister.

Flag: The Saltire, with a diagonal, X-shaped white cross on a blue field, is meant to represent the crucifixion of Scotland's patron saint, the apostle Andrew.

The Average Scot: The average Scottish person will live to age 79 and doesn't identify with an organized religion. He or she has free health care, gets 28 vacation days a year (versus 16 in the US), lives within a five-minute walk of a park or green space, and gets outdoors at least once a week.

lands and cities. Highlanders represented the stereotypical image of "true Scots," speaking Gaelic, wearing kilts, and playing bagpipes, while Lowlanders spoke languages of Saxon origin and wore trousers. After the Scottish Reformation, the Lowlanders embraced Protestantism, while most Highlanders stuck to Catholicism. Although this Lowlands/Highlands division has faded over time, some Scots still cling to it.

The Lowlands are dominated by a pair of rival cities: Edinburgh (on the east coast's Firth of Forth) and Glasgow (on the west

coast's Firth of Clyde) mark the endpoints of Scotland's 75-mile-long "Central Belt," where three-quarters of the country's population resides. Edinburgh, the old royal capital, teems with Scottish history and is the country's most popular tourist attraction. Glasgow, once a gloomy industrial city, is becoming a hip, laid-back city of art, music, and architecture. In addition to these two cities—both of which warrant a visit—the Lowlands' highlights include the medieval university town and golf mecca of St. Andrews, the small city of Stirling (with its castle and many nearby historic sites), and selected countryside stopovers.

Generally, the Highlands are hungry for the tourist dollar, and everything overtly Scottish is exploited to the kilt; you need to spend some time here to get to know the area's true character. You can get a feel for the Highlands with a quick drive to Oban, through Glencoe, then up the Caledonian Canal to Inverness. With more time, the Isles of Iona, Staffa, and Mull (an easy day trip from Oban); the Isle of Skye; the handy distillery town of Pit-

lochry; and countless brooding countryside castles will flesh out your Highlands experience. And for those really wanting to get off the beaten path, continue north—all the way up the dramatic west coast (called Wester Ross) to John O'Groats, at Britain's northeastern tip. To go farther, cross the Pentland Firth to Orkney, with its own unique culture and history.

At these northern latitudes, cold and drizzly weather isn't uncommon—even in midsummer. The blazing sun can quickly be covered over by black clouds and howling wind. Your B&B host will warn you to prepare for "four seasons in one day." Because Scots feel personally responsible for bad weather, they tend to be overly optimistic about forecasts. Take any Scottish promise of "sun by the afternoon" with a grain of salt—and bring your raincoat, just in case.

Americans and Canadians of Scottish descent enjoy coming "home" to Scotland. If you're Scottish, your surname will tell you which clan your ancestors likely belonged to. The prefix "Mac" (or "Mc") means "son of"—so "MacDonald" means the same thing as "Donaldson." Tourist shops everywhere are happy to help you track down your clan's tartan (distinctive plaid pattern). For more on how these "clan tartans" don't go back as far as you might think, see the sidebar on page 25.

Scotland shares a monarchy with the rest of the United Kingdom, though to Scots, Queen Elizabeth II is just "Queen Elizabeth"; the first Queen Elizabeth ruled England, but not Scotland. (In this book, I use England's numbering.) Scotland is not a sovereign state, but it is a "nation" in that it has its own traditions, ethnic identity, languages (Gaelic and Scots), and football league. To some extent, it even has its own government.

Recently, Scotland has enjoyed its greatest measure of political autonomy in centuries—a trend called "devolution." In

1999, the Scottish parliament convened in Edinburgh for the first time in almost 300 years; in 2004, it moved into its brand-new building near the foot of the Royal Mile. Though the Scottish parliament's powers are limited (most major decisions are still made in London), the Scots are enjoying the refreshing breeze of increased self-governance. In a 2014 independence referendum, the Scots favored staying in the United Kingdom by a margin of 10 percent. The question of independence will likely remain a pivotal issue in Scotland for many years to come.

Scotland even has its own currency...sort of. Scots use the same coins as England, Wales, and Northern Ireland, but Scotland also prints its own bills (featuring Scottish rather than English people and landmarks). Just to confuse tourists, three different banks print Scottish pound

SCOTLAND

notes, each with a different design. In the Lowlands (around Edinburgh and Glasgow), you'll receive both Scottish and English pounds from ATMs and in change. But in the Highlands, you'll almost never see English pounds. Bank of England notes are legal and widely used; Northern Ireland bank notes are legal but less common.

The Scottish flag—a diagonal, X-shaped white cross on a blue field—represents the cross of Scotland's patron saint, the Apostle Andrew (who was crucified on an X-shaped cross). You may not realize it, but you see the Scottish flag every time you look at the Union Jack: England's flag (the red St. George's cross on a white field) superimposed on Scotland's (a blue field with a white diagonal cross). The diagonal red cross (St. Patrick's cross)

British, Scottish, and English

Scotland and England have been tied together politically for more than 300 years, since the Act of Union in 1707. For a century and a half afterward, Scottish nationalists rioted for independence in Edinburgh's streets and led rebellions ("uprisings") in the Highlands. In this controversial union, history is clearly seen through two very different filters.

If you tour a British-oriented sight, such as Edinburgh's National War Museum Scotland, you'll find things told in a "happy union" way, which ignores the long history of Scottish resistance—from the ancient Picts through the time of Robert the Bruce. The official line: In 1706-1707, it was clear to England and certain parties in Scotland (especially landowners from the Lowlands) that it was in their mutual interest to dissolve the Scottish government and fold it into the United Kingdom, to be ruled from London.

But talk to a cabbie or your B&B host, and you may get a different spin. Scottish independence is still a hot-button issue. Since 2007, the Scottish National Party (SNP) has owned the largest majority in the Scottish Parliament. During a landmark referendum in September 2014, the Scots voted to remain part of the union—but many polls, right up until election day, suggested that things could easily have gone the other way.

The rift shows itself in sports, too. While the English may refer to a British team in international competition as "English," the Scots are careful to call it "British." If a Scottish athlete does well, the English call him "British." If he screws up… he's a clumsy Scot.

over Scotland's white one represents Northern Ireland. (Wales gets no love on the Union Jack.)

Here in "English-speaking" Scotland, you may still encounter a language barrier. First is the lovely, lilting Scottish accent—which may take you a while to understand. You may also hear an impenetrable dialect of Scottish English that many linguists consider to be a separate language, called "Scots." You may already know several Scots words: lad, lassie, wee, bonnie, glen, loch, aye. On menus, you'll see neeps and tatties (turnips and potatoes). And in place names, you'll see ben (mountain), brae (hill), firth (estuary), and kyle (strait). Second is Gaelic (pronounced "gallic" here; Ireland's closely related Celtic language is pronounced "gaylic")—the ancient Celtic language of the Scots. While only one percent of the population speaks Gaelic, it's making a comeback—particularly in the remote and traditional Highlands.

While soccer ("football") is as popular here as anywhere, golf is Scotland's other national sport. But in Scotland, it's not neces-

SCOTLAND

sarily considered an exclusively upper-class pursuit; you can generally play a round at a basic course for about £15. While Scotland's best scenery is along the west coast, its best golfing is on the east coast—home to many prestigious golf courses. Most of these are links courses, which use natural sand from the beaches for the bunkers. For tourists, these links are more authentic, more challenging, and more fun than the regular-style courses (with artificial landforms) farther inland. If you're a golfer, St. Andrews—on the east coast—is a pilgrimage worth making.

Outside of the main cities, Scotland's sights are subtle, but its misty glens, brooding countryside castles, and warm culture are plenty engaging. Whether toasting with beer, whisky, or Scotland's favorite soft drink, Irn-Bru, enjoy meeting the Scottish people. It's easy to fall in love with the irrepressible spirit and beautiful landscape of this faraway corner of Britain.

EDINBURGH

Edinburgh is the historical, cultural, and political capital of Scotland. For nearly a thousand years, Scotland's kings, parliaments, writers, thinkers, and bankers have called Edinburgh home. Today, it remains Scotland's most sophisticated city.

Edinburgh (ED'n-burah—only tourists pronounce it like "Pittsburgh") is Scotland's showpiece and one of Europe's most entertaining cities. It's a place of stunning vistas—nestled among craggy bluffs and studded with a prickly skyline of spires, towers, domes, and steeples. Proud statues of famous Scots dot the urban landscape. The buildings are a harmonious yellow-gray, all built from the same local sandstone.

Culturally, Edinburgh has always been the place where Lowland culture (urban and English) met Highland style (rustic and Gaelic). Tourists will find no end of traditional Scottish clichés: whisky tastings, kilt shops, bagpipe-playing buskers, and gimmicky tours featuring Scotland's bloody history and ghost stories.

Edinburgh is two cities in one. The Old Town stretches along the Royal Mile, from the grand castle on top to the palace on the bottom. Along this colorful labyrinth of cobbled streets and narrow lanes, medieval skyscrapers stand shoulder to shoulder, hiding peaceful courtyards.

A few hundred yards north of the Old Town lies the New Town. It's a magnificent planned neighborhood (from the 1700s). Here, you'll enjoy upscale shops, broad boulevards, straight streets, square squares, circular circuses, and Georgian mansions decked out in Greek-style columns and statues.

Today's Edinburgh is big in banking, scientific research, and scholarship at its four universities. Since 1999, when Scotland regained a measure of self-rule, Edinburgh reassumed its place as home of the Scottish Parliament. The city hums with life. Students and professionals pack the pubs and art galleries. It's especially lively in August, when the Edinburgh Festival takes over the town. Historic, monumental, fun, and well organized, Edinburgh is a tourist's delight.

PLANNING YOUR TIME

While the major sights can be seen in a day, I'd give Edinburgh two days and three nights.

Day 1: Tour the castle, then consider catching a city bus tour for a one-hour loop (departing from a block below the castle at the Hub/Tolbooth Church; you could munch a sandwich from the top deck if you're into multitasking). Back near the castle, take my self-guided Royal Mile walk, stopping in at shops and museums that interest you (Gladstone's Land is tops but you can only visit it by booking a tour). At the bottom of the Mile, consider visiting the Scottish Parliament, the Palace of Holyroodhouse, or both. If the weather's good, you could hike back to your B&B along the Salisbury Crags.

Day 2: Visit the National Museum of Scotland. After lunch (several great choices nearby, on Forrest Road), stroll through the Princes Street Gardens and the Scottish National Gallery. Then follow my self-guided walk through the New Town, visiting the Scottish National Portrait Gallery and the Georgian House—or squeeze in a quick tour of the good ship *Britannia* (check last entry time before you head out).

Evenings: Options include various "haunted Edinburgh" walks, literary pub crawls, or live music in pubs. Sadly, full-blown traditional folk performances are just about extinct, surviving only in excruciatingly schmaltzy variety shows put on for tour-bus groups. Perhaps the most authentic evening out is just settling down in a pub to sample the whisky and local beers while meeting the locals...and attempting to understand them through their thick Scottish accents (see "Nightlife in Edinburgh," page 94).

Orientation to Edinburgh

A VERBAL MAP

With 490,000 people (835,000 in the metro area), Edinburgh is Scotland's second-biggest city (after Glasgow). But the tourist's Edinburgh is compact: Old Town, New Town, and the B&B area south of the city center.

Edinburgh's **Old Town** stretches across a ridgeline slung between two bluffs. From west to east, this "Royal Mile" runs from the Castle Rock—which is visible from anywhere—to the base of the 822-foot extinct volcano called Arthur's Seat. For visitors, this east-west axis is the center of the action. Just south of the Royal Mile are the university and the National Museum of Scotland; farther to the south is a handy B&B neighborhood that lines up along **Dalkeith Road** and **Mayfield Gardens.** North of the Royal Mile ridge is the **New Town,** a neighborhood of grid-planned streets and elegant Georgian buildings.

In the center of it all—in a drained lake bed between the Old and New Towns—sit the Princes Street Gardens park and Waverley Bridge, where you'll find the Waverley train station, TI, Waverley Mall, bus info office (starting point for most city bus tours), Scottish National Gallery, and a covered dance-and-music pavilion.

EDINBURGH

TOURIST INFORMATION

The crowded TI is as central as can be, on the rooftop of the Waverley Mall and Waverley train station (Mon-Sat 9:00-17:00, Sun from 10:00, June daily until 18:00, July-Aug daily until 19:00; tel. 0131-473-3868, www.visitscotland.com). While the staff is helpful, be warned that much of their information is skewed by tourism payola (and booking seats on bus tours seems to be a big priority). There's also a TI at the airport (tel. 0131-344-3120).

For more information than what's included in the TI's free map, buy the excellent *Collins Discovering Edinburgh* map (which comes with opinionated commentary and locates almost every major sight). If you're interested in evening music, ask for the comprehensive entertainment listing, *The List.* Also consider buying Historic Scotland's Explorer Pass, which can save you some money if you visit the castles at both Edinburgh and Stirling, or are also visiting the Orkney Islands.

ARRIVAL IN EDINBURGH

By Train: Arriving by train at Waverley Station puts you in the city center and below the TI. Taxis line up outside, on Market Street or Waverley Bridge. For the TI or bus stop, follow signs for Princes Street and ride up several escalators. From here, the TI is to your left, and the city bus stop is two blocks to your right (for bus directions from here to my recommended B&Bs, see "Sleeping in Edinburgh," later).

By Bus: Scottish Citylink, Megabus, and National Express buses use the bus station (with luggage lockers) in the New Town, two blocks north of the train station on St. Andrew Square.

EDINBURGH

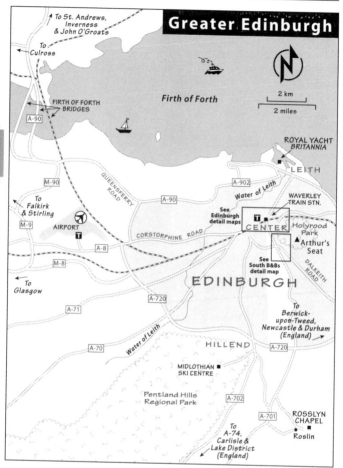

By Car: If you're arriving from the north, rather than drive through downtown Edinburgh to my recommended B&Bs, circle the city on the A-720 City Bypass road. Approaching Edinburgh on the M-9, take the M-8 (direction: Glasgow) and quickly get onto the A-720 City Bypass (direction: Edinburgh South). After four miles, you'll hit a roundabout. Ignore signs directing you into *Edinburgh North* and stay on the A-720 for 10 more miles to the next and last roundabout, named *Sheriffhall*. Exit the roundabout at the first left *(A-7 Edinburgh)*. From here it's four miles to the B&B neighborhood. After a while, the A-7 becomes Dalkeith Road (you'll pass the Royal Infirmary hospital complex). If you see the huge Royal Commonwealth Pool, you've gone a couple of blocks too far (avoid this by referring to the map on page 98).

If you're driving in on the A-68 from the south, first follow signs for *Edinburgh South & West* (A-720), then exit at *A-7(N)/Edinburgh* and follow the directions above.

By Plane: Edinburgh's airport is eight miles and a 25-minute taxi ride from downtown. For information, see "Edinburgh Connections," at the end of this chapter.

HELPFUL HINTS

Sunday Activities: Many Royal Mile sights close on Sunday (except in Aug), but other major sights and shops are open. Sunday is a good day to catch a guided walking tour along the Royal Mile or a city bus tour (buses go faster in light traffic). The slopes of Arthur's Seat are lively with hikers and picnickers on weekends.

Festivals: August is a crowded, popular month to visit Edinburgh thanks to the multiple festivals hosted here, including the official Edinburgh International Festival, the Fringe Festival, and the Military Tattoo. Book ahead for hotels, events, and restaurant dinners if you'll be visiting in August, and expect to pay significantly more for your room. Many museums and shops have extended hours in August. For more festival details, see page 87.

Baggage Storage: At the train station, you'll find pricey, high-security luggage storage near platform 2 (daily 7:00-23:00). There are also lockers at the bus station on St. Andrew Square, just two blocks north of the train station.

Laundry: The **Ace Cleaning Centre** launderette is located near my recommended B&Bs south of town. You can pay for full-service laundry (drop off in the morning for same-day service) or stay and do it yourself. For a small extra fee, they'll collect your laundry from your B&B and drop it off the next day (Mon-Fri 8:00-20:00, Sat 9:00-17:00, Sun 10:00-16:00, along bus route to city center at 13 South Clerk Street, opposite Queens Hall, tel. 0131/667-0549).

Bike Rental and Tours: The laid-back crew at **Cycle Scotland** happily recommends good bike routes with your rental (prices starting at £20/3 hours or £30/day, electric bikes available for extra fee, daily 10:00-18:00, may close for a couple of months in winter, just off Royal Mile at 29 Blackfriars Street, tel. 0131/556-5560, mobile 07796-886-899, www.cyclescotland.co.uk, Peter). They also run guided three-hour bike tours daily at 11:00 that start on the Royal Mile and ride through Holyrood Park, Arthur's Seat, Duddingston Village, Doctor Neil's (Secret) Garden, and along the Innocent railway path (£45/person, extra fee for e-bike, book ahead).

Car Rental: These places have offices both in the town center and at the airport: **Avis** (24 East London Street, tel. 0844-544-6059,

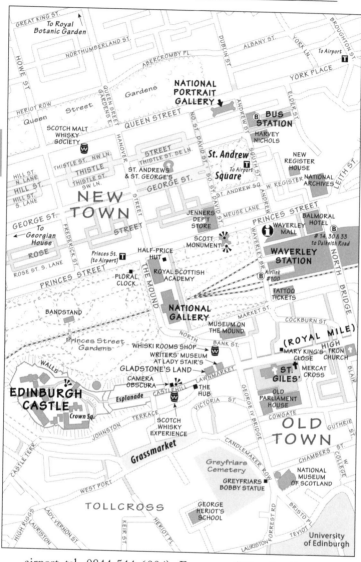

airport tel. 0844-544-6004), **Europcar** (Waverley Station, near platform 2, tel. 0871-384-3453, airport tel. 0871-384-3406), **Hertz** (10 Picardy Place, tel. 0843-309-3026, airport tel. 0843-309-3025), and **Budget** (24 East London Street, tel. 0844-544-9064, airport tel. 0844-544-4605). Some downtown offices close or have reduced hours on Sunday, but the airport locations tend to be open daily. If you plan to rent a car, pick it up on your way out of Edinburgh—you won't need it in town.

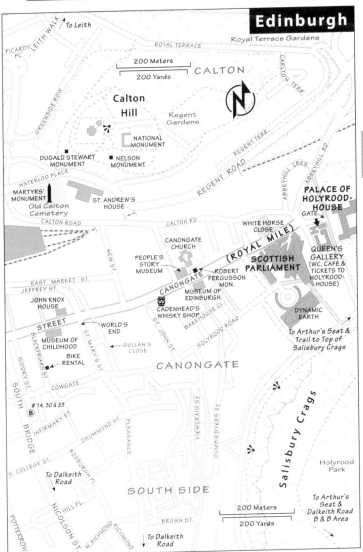

Dress for the Weather: Weather blows in and out—bring your sweater and be prepared for rain.

GETTING AROUND EDINBURGH

Many of Edinburgh's sights are within walking distance of one another, but **buses** come in handy—especially if you're staying at a B&B south of the city center. Double-decker buses come with fine views upstairs. It's easy once you get the hang of it: Buses come by frequently (screens at bus stops show wait times) and have free, fast

Edinburgh at a Glance

▲▲▲**Royal Mile** Historic road—good for walking—stretching from the castle down to the palace, lined with museums, pubs, and shops. **Hours:** Always open, but best during business hours, with walking tours daily. See page 23.

▲▲▲**Edinburgh Castle** Iconic hilltop fort and royal residence complete with crown jewels, Romanesque chapel, memorial, and fine military museum. **Hours:** Daily 9:30-18:00, Oct-March until 17:00. See page 45.

▲▲▲**National Museum of Scotland** Intriguing, well-displayed artifacts from prehistoric times to the 20th century. **Hours:** Daily 10:00-17:00. See page 67.

▲▲**Gladstone's Land** Seventeenth-century Royal Mile merchant's residence. **Hours:** Daily 10:30-16:00 by tour only, closed Nov-March. See page 56.

▲▲**St. Giles' Cathedral** Preaching grounds of Scottish Reformer John Knox, with spectacular organ, Neo-Gothic chapel, and distinctive crown spire. **Hours:** Mon-Fri 9:00-19:00, Sat until 17:00; Oct-April Mon-Sat 9:00-17:00; Sun 13:00-17:00 year-round. See page 57.

▲▲**Scottish Parliament Building** Striking headquarters for parliament, which returned to Scotland in 1999. **Hours:** Mon-Sat 10:00-17:00, longer hours Tue-Thu when parliament is in session (Sept-June), closed Sun year-round. See page 64.

▲▲**Palace of Holyroodhouse** The Queen's splendid official residence in Scotland, with lavish rooms, 12th-century abbey, and gallery with rotating exhibits. **Hours:** Daily April-Oct 9:30-18:00, Nov-March until 16:30, closed during royal visits. See page 65.

▲▲**Scottish National Gallery** Choice sampling of European masters and Scotland's finest. **Hours:** Daily 10:00-17:00, Thu until 19:00; longer hours in Aug. See page 71.

▲▲**Scottish National Portrait Gallery** Beautifully displayed

Wi-Fi on board. The only hassle is that you must pay with exact change (£1.60/ride, £4/all-day pass). As you board, tell your driver where you're going (or just say "single ticket") and drop your change into the box. Ping the bell as you near your stop. You can pick up a route map at the TI or at the transit office at the Old Town end of Waverley Bridge (tel. 0131/555-6363, www.lothianbuses.com).

Who's Who of Scottish history. **Hours:** Daily 10:00-17:00. See page 76.

▲▲**Georgian House** Intimate peek at upper-crust life in the late 1700s. **Hours:** Daily 10:00-17:00, March and Nov 11:00-16:00, closed Dec-Feb. See page 79.

▲▲**Royal Yacht** *Britannia* Ship for the royal family with a history of distinguished passengers, a 15-minute trip out of town. **Hours:** Daily 9:30-16:30, Oct until 16:00, Nov-March 10:00-15:30 (these are last-entry times). See page 79.

▲**Scotch Whisky Experience** Gimmicky but fun and educational introduction to Scotland's most famous beverage. **Hours:** Generally daily 10:00-18:00. See page 55.

▲**The Real Mary King's Close** Tour of underground street and houses last occupied in the 17th century, viewable by guided tour. **Hours:** Daily 10:00-21:00, Nov-March Sun-Thu until 17:00 (these are last-tour times). See page 62.

▲**Museum of Childhood** Five stories of historic fun. **Hours:** Thu-Mon 10:00-17:00 except Sun from 12:00, closed Tue-Wed. See page 62.

▲**People's Story Museum** Everyday life from the 18th to 20th century. **Hours:** Wed-Sat 10:00-17:00 except Sun from 12:00, closed Mon-Tue. See page 63.

▲**Museum of Edinburgh** Historic mementos, from the original National Covenant inscribed on animal skin to early golf balls. **Hours:** Thu-Mon 10:00-17:00 except Sun from 12:00, closed Tue-Wed. See page 63.

▲**Rosslyn Chapel** Small 15th-century church chock-full of intriguing carvings a short drive outside of Edinburgh. **Hours:** Mon-Sat 9:30-17:00, June-Aug until 18:00, Sun 12:00-16:45 year-round. See page 81.

EDINBURGH

Edinburgh's single **tram** line (also £1.60/ride) is designed more for locals than tourists; it's most useful for reaching the airport (see "Edinburgh Connections" at the end of this chapter).

The 1,300 **taxis** cruising Edinburgh's streets are easy to flag down (ride between downtown and the B&B neighborhood costs about £7; rates go up after 18:00 and on weekends). They can turn on a dime, so hail them in either direction. **Uber** also works well here.

Tours in Edinburgh

Royal Mile Walking Tours

Walking tours are an Edinburgh specialty; you'll see groups trailing entertaining guides all over town. Below I've listed good all-purpose walks; for **literary pub crawls** and **ghost tours,** see "Nightlife in Edinburgh" on page 94.

Edinburgh Tour Guides offers a good historical walk (without all the ghosts and goblins). Their Royal Mile tour is a gentle two-hour downhill stroll from the castle to the palace (£16.50; daily at 9:30 and 19:00; meet outside Gladstone's Land, near the top of the Royal Mile—see map on page 26, must reserve ahead, mobile 0785-888-0072, www.edinburghtourguides.com, info@ edinburghtourguides.com).

Mercat Tours offers a 1.5-hour "Secrets of the Royal Mile" walk that's more entertaining than intellectual (£13; £30 includes optional, 45-minute guided Edinburgh Castle visit; daily at 10:00 and 13:00, leaves from Mercat Cross on the Royal Mile, tel. 0131/225-5445, www.mercattours.com). The guides, who enjoy making a short story long, ignore the big sights and take you behind the scenes with piles of barely historical gossip, bully-pulpit Scottish pride, and fun but forgettable trivia. They also offer other tours, such as ghost walks, tours of 18th-century underground vaults on the southern slope of the Royal Mile, and *Outlander* sights (see their website for a rundown).

Sandemans New Edinburgh runs "free" tours multiple times a day; you won't pay upfront, but the guide will expect a tip (check schedule online, 3 hours, meet in front of Starbucks by Tron Kirk on High Street, www.neweuropetours.eu).

The **Voluntary Guides Association** offers free two-hour walks, but only during the Edinburgh Festival. You don't need a reservation—just show up (check website for times, generally depart from City Chambers across from St. Giles' Cathedral on the Royal Mile, www.edinburghfestivalguides.org). You can also hire their guides (for a small fee) for private tours outside of festival time.

Blue Badge Local Guides

The following guides charge similar prices and offer half-day and full-day tours: **Jean Blair** (a delightful teacher and guide, £190/ day without car, £430/day with car, mobile 0798-957-0287, www. travelthroughscotland.com, scotguide7@gmail.com); **Sergio La Spina** (an Argentinean who adopted Edinburgh as his hometown more than 20 years ago, £250/day, tel. 0131/664-1731, mobile 0797-330-6579, www.vivaescocia.com, sergiolaspina@aol.com); **Ken Hanley** (who wears his kilt as if pants don't exist, £130/half-day, £250/day, extra charge if he uses his car—seats up to six, tel. 0131/666-1944, mobile 0771-034-2044, www.small-world-tours. co.uk, kennethhanley@me.com); and **Liz Everett** (walking tours only—no car; £165/half-day, £230/day, mobile 07821-683-837, liz. everett@live.co.uk).

Hop-On, Hop-Off Bus Tours

The following one-hour hop-on, hop-off bus tour routes, all run by the same company, circle the town center, stopping at the major

sights. **Edinburgh Tour** (green buses) focuses on the city center, with live guides. **City Sightseeing** (red buses, focuses on Old Town) has recorded commentary, as does the **Majestic Tour** (blue-and-yellow buses, includes a stop at the *Britannia* and Royal Botanic Garden). You can pay for just one tour (£15/24 hours), but most people pay a few pounds more for a ticket covering all buses (£20; buses run April-Oct roughly 9:00-19:00, shorter hours off-season; every 10-15 minutes, buy tickets on board, tel. 0131/220-0770, www.edinburghtour.com). On sunny days the buses go topless, but come with increased traffic noise and exhaust fumes. For £52, the Royal Edinburgh Ticket covers two days of unlimited travel on all three buses, as well as admission (and line-skipping privileges) at Edinburgh Castle, the Palace of Holyroodhouse, and *Britannia* (www.royaledinburghticket.co.uk).

The **3 Bridges Tour** combines a hop-on, hop-off bus to South Queensferry with a boat tour on the Firth of Forth (£20, 3 hours total).

Weekend Tour Packages for Students

Andy Steves (Rick's son) runs Weekend Student Adventures (WSA Europe), offering 3-day and 10-day budget travel packages across Europe including accommodations, skip-the-line sightseeing, and unique local experiences. Locally guided and DIY options are available for student and budget travelers in 13 of Europe's most popular cities, including Edinburgh (guided trips from €199, see www.wsaeurope.com for details). Check out Andy's tips, resources, and podcast at www.andysteves.com.

EDINBURGH

Day Trips from Edinburgh

Many companies run a variety of day trips to regional sights, as well as multiday and themed itineraries. (Several of the local guides listed earlier have cars, too.)

The most popular tour is the all-day **Highlands trip.** The standard Highlands tour gives those with limited time a chance to experience the wonders of Scotland's wild and legend-soaked Highlands in a single long day (about £50, roughly 8:00-20:00). Itineraries vary but you'll generally visit/pass through the Trossachs, Rannoch Moor, Glencoe, Fort William, Fort Augustus on Loch Ness (some tours offer an optional boat ride), and Pitlochry. To save time, look for a tour that gives you a short glimpse of Loch Ness rather than driving its entire length or doing a boat trip. (Once you've seen a little of it, you've seen it all.)

Larger outfits, typically using bigger buses, include **Timberbush Highland Tours** (tel. 0131/226-6066, www. timberbushtours.com), **Gray Line** (tel. 0131/555-5558, www. graylinescotland.com), **Highland Experience** (tel. 0131/226-1414, www.highlandexperience.com), **Highland Explorer** (tel. 0131/558-3738, www.highlandexplorertours.com), and **Scotline** (tel. 0131/557-0162, www.scotlinetours.co.uk). Other companies pride themselves on keeping group sizes small, with 16-seat minibuses; these include **Rabbie's** (tel. 0131/212-5005, www.rabbies. com) and **Heart of Scotland Tours: The Wee Red Bus** (10 percent Rick Steves discount on full-price day tours—mention when booking, does not apply to overnight tours or senior/student rates, occasionally canceled off-season if too few sign up—leave a contact number, tel. 0131/228-2888, www.heartofscotlandtours.co.uk, run by Nick Roche).

For young backpackers, **Haggis Adventures** runs day tours plus overnight trips of up to 10 days (tel. 0131/557-9393, www. haggisadventures.com).

At **Discreet Scotland,** Matthew Wight and his partners specialize in tours of greater Edinburgh and Scotland in spacious SUVs—good for families (£360/2 people, 8 hours, mobile 0798-941-6990, www.discreetscotland.com).

Walks in Edinburgh

I've outlined two walks in Edinburgh: along the Royal Mile, and through the New Town. Many of the sights we'll pass on these walks are described in more detail later, under "Sights in Edinburgh."

THE ROYAL MILE

The Royal Mile is one of Europe's most interesting historic walks—it's worth ▲▲▲. The following self-guided stroll is also available as a 🎧 downloadable Rick Steves audio tour; see page 125.

Overview

Start at Edinburgh Castle at the top and amble down to the Palace of Holyroodhouse. Along the way, the street changes names—Castlehill, Lawnmarket, High Street, and Canongate—but it's a straight, downhill shot totaling just over one mile. And nearly every step is packed with shops, cafés, and lanes leading to tiny squares.

The city of Edinburgh was born on the easily defended rock at the top, where the castle stands today. Celtic tribes (and maybe the Romans) once occupied this site. As the town grew, it spilled downhill along the sloping ridge that became the Royal Mile. Because this strip of land is so narrow, there was no place to build but up. So in medieval times, it was densely packed with multistory "tenements"—large edifices under one roof that housed a number of tenants.

As you walk, you'll be tracing the growth of the city—its birth atop Castle Hill, its Old Town heyday in the 1600s, its expansion in the 1700s into the Georgian New Town (leaving the old quarter an overcrowded, disease-ridden Victorian slum), and on to the 21st century at the modern Scottish parliament building (2004).

In parts, the Royal Mile feels like one long Scottish shopping mall, selling all manner of kitschy souvenirs (known locally as "tartan tat"), shortbread, and whisky. But the streets are also packed with history, and if you push past the postcard racks into one of the many side alleys, you can still find a few surviving rough edges of the old city. Despite the drizzle, be sure to look up—spires, carvings, and towering Gothic "skyscrapers" give this city its unique urban identity.

This walk covers the Royal Mile's landmarks, but skips the many museums and indoor attractions along the way. These and other sights are described in walking order under "Sights in Edinburgh" on page 45. You can stay focused on the walk (which takes about 1.5 hours, without entering sights), then return later to visit the various indoor attractions; or review the sight descriptions beforehand and pop into those that interest you as you pass them.

• *We'll start at the Castle Esplanade, the big parking lot at the entrance to...*

❶ Edinburgh Castle

Edinburgh was born on the bluff—a big rock—where the castle now stands. Since before recorded history, people have lived on this strategic, easily defended perch.

The **castle** is an imposing symbol of Scottish independence. Flanking the entryway are statues of the fierce warriors who battled English invaders, William Wallace (on the right) and Robert the Bruce (left). Between them is the Scottish motto, *Nemo me impune lacessit*—roughly, "No one messes with me and gets away with it." (For a self-guided tour of Edinburgh Castle, see page 46.)

The esplanade—built as a military parade ground (1816)—is now the site of the annual Military Tattoo. This spectacular massing of regimental bands fills the square nightly for most of August. Fans watch from temporary bleacher seats to see kilt-wearing bagpipers marching against the spectacular backdrop of the castle. TV crews broadcast the spectacle to all corners of the globe.

When the bleachers aren't up, there are fine views in both directions from the esplanade. Facing north, you'll see the body of water called the Firth of Forth, and Fife beyond that. (The Firth of Forth is the estuary where the River Forth flows into the North Sea.) Still facing north, find the lacy spire of the Scott Monument and two Neoclassical buildings housing art galleries. Beyond them, the stately buildings of Edinburgh's New Town rise. (For a self-guided walk of the New Town, see page 38.) Panning to the right, find the Nelson Monument and some faux Greek ruins atop Calton Hill (see page 85).

The city's many bluffs, crags, and ridges were built up by volcanoes, then carved down by glaciers—a city formed in "fire and ice," as the locals say. So, during the Ice Age, as a river of glaciers swept in from the west (behind today's castle), it ran into the super-hard volcanic basalt of Castle Rock and flowed around it, cutting valleys on either side and leaving a tail that became the Royal Mile you're about to walk.

At the bottom of the esplanade, where the square hits the road, look left to find a plaque on the wall above the tiny **witches' well** (now a planter). This memorializes 300 women who were accused of witchcraft and burned here. Below was the Nor' Loch, the swampy lake where those accused of witchcraft (mostly women) were tested: Bound up, they were dropped into the lake. If they

The Kilt

The kilt, Scotland's national dress, is intimately tied to the country's history. The six-foot-by-nine-foot bolt of fabric originated in the 1500s as a multipurpose robe, toga, tent, poncho, and ground cloth. A wearer would lay it on the ground to scrunch up pleats, then wrap it around the waist and belt it. Extra fabric was thrown over the shoulder or tucked into the belt, creating both a rakish sash and a rucksack-like pouch.

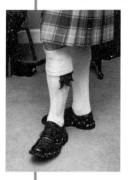

The kilt was standard Highlands dress and became a patriotic statement during conflicts with England. After the tragic-for-Scotland Battle of Culloden in 1746, the British government wanted to end the Scottish clan system. Wearing the kilt, speaking Gaelic, and playing the bagpipes were all outlawed.

In 1782, kilts were permitted again, but had taken on an unrefined connotation, so many Scots no longer wanted to wear one. This changed in 1822 when King George IV visited Edinburgh, wearing a kilt to send the message that he was king of Scotland. Scottish aristocrats were charmed by the king's pageantry, and the kilt was in vogue once more.

During the king's visit, Sir Walter Scott organized a Highland festival that also helped change the image of traditional Scottish culture, giving it a newfound respectability. A generation later, Queen Victoria raised the image of Scottish culture even higher. She loved Scotland and wallpapered her palace at Balmoral with tartan patterns.

The colors and patterns of the original kilts were determined by what dyes were available and who wove them. Because members of one clan tended to live in the same areas, they often wore similar patterns—but the colors were muted, and the patterns weren't necessarily designed to represent a single clan. The "clan tartans" you'll see in Scottish souvenir shops—with a specific, brightly colored design for each family—started as a scam by fabric salesmen in Victorian times. Since then, tartanry has been embraced as if it were historic. (By the way, Scots use these key terms differently than Americans do: "Tartan" is the pattern itself, while "plaid" is the piece of cloth worn over the shoulder with a kilt.)

As Highlanders moved to cities and took jobs in factories, the smaller kilt, or philibeg, replaced the traditional kilt, which could become dangerously snagged by modern machinery. Half the weight of old-style kilts, the practical philibeg is more like a wraparound skirt.

Other kilt-related gear includes the sporran, the leather pouch worn around the waist, and the *sgian dubh* ("black knife"), the short blade worn in the top of the sock. If you're in the market for a kilt, see page 92.

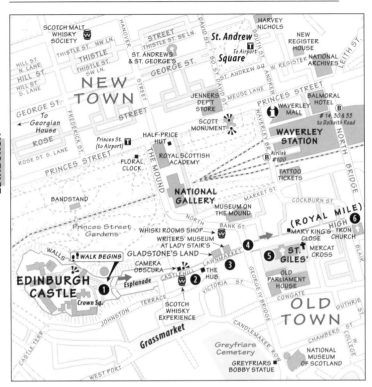

sank and drowned, they were innocent. If they floated, they were guilty, and were burned here in front of the castle, providing the city folk a nice afternoon out. The plaque shows two witches: one good and one bad. Tickle the serpent's snout to sympathize with the witches. (I just made that up.)

• *Start walking down the Royal Mile. The first block is a street called...*

❷ Castlehill

You're immediately in the tourist hubbub. The big tank-like building on your left was the Old Town's **reservoir.** You'll see the wellheads it served all along this walk. While it once held 1.5 million gallons of water, today it's filled with the touristy Tartan Weaving Mill and Exhibition. While it's interesting to see the mill at work, you'll have to twist your way down through several floors of tartanry and Chinese-produced Scottish kitsch to reach it at the bottom level.

The black-and-white tower ahead on the

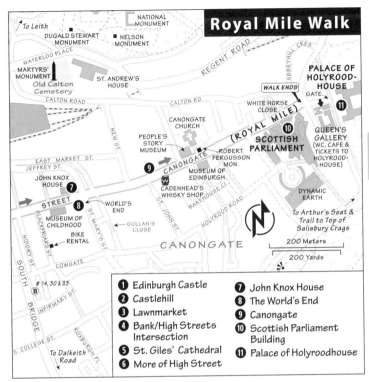

Royal Mile Walk

- To Leith
- NATIONAL MONUMENT
- DUGALD STEWART MONUMENT
- NELSON MONUMENT
- REGENT ROAD
- ABBEYHILL CRES.
- WATERLOO PLACE
- MARTYRS' MONUMENT
- Old Calton Cemetery
- ST. ANDREW'S HOUSE
- CALTON RD.
- WALK ENDS
- PALACE OF HOLYROOD-HOUSE
- GATE
- CALTON ROAD
- WHITE HORSE CLOSE
- QUEEN'S GALLERY (WC, CAFE & TICKETS TO HOLYROOD-HOUSE)
- CANONGATE CHURCH
- (ROYAL MILE)
- SCOTTISH PARLIAMENT
- NEW ST.
- EAST MARKET ST.
- PEOPLE'S STORY MUSEUM
- ROBERT FERGUSSON MON.
- CANONGATE
- MUSEUM OF EDINBURGH
- JEFFREY ST.
- JOHN KNOX HOUSE
- CADENHEAD'S WHISKY SHOP
- BAKEHOUSE CL.
- DYNAMIC EARTH
- STREET
- WORLD'S END
- ST. JOHN'S ST.
- HOLYROOD ROAD
- BLACKFRIARS ST.
- MUSEUM OF CHILDHOOD
- GULLAN'S CLOSE
- ST. MARY'S ST.
- To Arthur's Seat & Trail to Top of Salisbury Crags
- BIKE RENTAL
- NIDDRY ST.
- CANONGATE
- 200 Meters
- COWGATE
- 200 Yards
- SOUTH BRIDGE
- # 14, 30 & 33
- B
- INFIRMARY ST.
- S. COLLEGE ST.
- ROXBURGH PL.
- To Dalkeith Road
- EDINBURGH (side tab)

1. Edinburgh Castle
2. Castlehill
3. Lawnmarket
4. Bank/High Streets Intersection
5. St. Giles' Cathedral
6. More of High Street
7. John Knox House
8. The World's End
9. Canongate
10. Scottish Parliament Building
11. Palace of Holyroodhouse

left has entertained visitors since the 1850s with its **camera obscura,** a darkened room where a mirror and a series of lenses capture live images of the city surroundings outside. (Giggle at the funny mirrors as you walk fatly by.) Across the street, filling the old Castlehill Primary School, is a gimmicky-if-intoxicating whisky-sampling exhibit called the **Scotch Whisky Experience** (a.k.a. "Malt Disney"). Both of these are described later, under "Sights in Edinburgh."

• *Just ahead, in front of the church with the tall, lacy spire, is the old market square known as...*

❸ Lawnmarket

During the Royal Mile's heyday, in the 1600s, this intersection was bigger and served as a market for fabric (especially "lawn," a linen-like cloth). The market would fill this space with hustle, bustle, and lots of commerce. The round white hump in the middle of the roundabout is all that remains of the official weighing beam called the Butter Tron—where all goods sold were weighed for honesty and tax purposes.

Towering above Lawnmarket, with the tallest spire in the

city, is the former **Tolbooth Church.** This impressive Neo-Gothic structure (1844) is now home to the Hub, Edinburgh's festival-ticket and information center. The world-famous Edinburgh Festival fills the month of August with cultural action. The various festivals feature classical music, traditional and fringe theater (especially comedy), art, books, and more. Drop inside the building to get festival info (see also page 87). This is a handy stop for its WC, café, and free Wi-Fi.

In the 1600s, this—along with the next stretch, called High Street—was the city's main street. At that time, Edinburgh was bursting with breweries, printing presses, and banks. Tens of thousands of citizens were squeezed into the narrow confines of the Old Town. Here on this ridge, they built **tenements** (multiple-unit residences) similar to the more recent ones you see today. These tenements, rising 10 stories and more, were some of the tallest domestic buildings in Europe. The living arrangements shocked class-conscious English visitors to Edinburgh because the tenements were occupied by rich and poor alike—usually the poor in the cellars and attics, and the rich in the middle floors.

• *Continue a half-block down the Mile.*

Gladstone's Land (at #477b, on the left), a surviving original tenement, was acquired by a wealthy merchant in 1617. Stand in front of the building and look up at this centuries-old skyscraper. This design was standard for its time: a shop or shops on the ground floor, with columns and an arcade, and residences on the floors above. Because window glass was expensive, the lower halves of window openings were made of cheaper wood, which swung out like shutters for ventilation—and were convenient for tossing out garbage. (Gladstone's Land can be seen by tour only and is closed Nov-March—consider dropping in and booking ahead for

a spot. For details, see listing on page 56.) Out front, you may also see trainers with live birds of prey. While this is mostly just a fun way to show off for tourists (and raise donations for the Just Falconry center), docents explain the connection: The building's owner was named Thomas Gledstanes—and *gled* is the Scots word for "hawk."

Branching off the spine of the

Royal Mile are a number of narrow alleyways that go by various local names. A "wynd" (rhymes with "kind") is a narrow, winding lane. A "pend" is an arched gateway. "Gate" is from an Old Norse word for street. And a "close" is a tiny alley between two buildings (originally with a door that "closed" at night). A "close" usually leads to a "court," or courtyard.

To explore one of these alleyways, head into **Lady Stair's Close** (on the left, 10 steps downhill from Gladstone's Land). This alley pops out in a small courtyard, where you'll find the **Writers' Museum** (described on page 56). It's well worth a visit for fans of Scotland's holy trinity of writers (Robert Burns, Sir Walter Scott, and Robert Louis Stevenson), but it's also a free glimpse of what a typical home might have looked like in the 1600s. Burns actually lived for a while in this neighborhood, in 1786, when he first arrived in Edinburgh.

Opposite Gladstone's Land (at #322), another close leads to **Riddle's Court.** Wander through here and imagine Edinburgh in the 17th and 18th centuries, when tourists came here to marvel at its skyscrapers. Some 40,000 people were jammed into the few blocks between here and the World's End pub (which we'll reach soon). Visualize the labyrinthine maze of the old city, with people scurrying through these back alleyways, buying and selling, and popping into taverns.

No city in Europe was as densely populated—or perhaps as filthy. Without modern hygiene, it was a living hell of smoke, stench, and noise, with the constant threat of fire, collapse, and disease. The dirt streets were soiled with sewage from bedpans emptied out windows. By the 1700s, the Old Town was rife with poverty and cholera outbreaks. The smoky home fires rising from tenements and the infamous smell (or "reek" in Scottish) that wafted across the city gave it a nickname that sticks today: "Auld Reekie."

• *Return to the Royal Mile and continue down it a few steps to take in some sights at the...*

❹ Bank/High Streets Intersection

A number of sights cluster here, where Lawnmarket changes its name to High Street and intersects with Bank Street and George IV Bridge.

Begin with **Deacon Brodie's Tavern.** Read the "Doctor Jekyll and Mr. Hyde" story of this pub's

EDINBURGH

notorious namesake on the wall facing Bank Street. Then, to see his spooky split personality, check out both sides of the hanging signpost. Brodie—a pillar of the community by day but a burglar by night—epitomizes the divided personality of 1700s Edinburgh. It was a rich, productive city—home to great philosophers and scientists, who actively contributed to the Enlightenment. Meanwhile, the Old Town was riddled with crime and squalor. The city was scandalized when a respected surgeon—driven by a passion for medical research and needing corpses—was accused of colluding with two lowlifes, named Burke and Hare, to acquire freshly murdered corpses for dissection. (In the next century, in the late 1800s, novelist Robert Louis Stevenson would capture the dichotomy of Edinburgh's rich-poor society in his *Strange Case of Dr. Jekyll and Mr. Hyde.*)

In the late 1700s, Edinburgh's upper class moved out of the Old Town into a planned community called the New Town (a quarter-mile north of here). Eventually, most tenements were torn down and replaced with newer **Victorian buildings.** You'll see some at this intersection.

Look left down Bank Street to the green-domed **Bank of Scotland.** This was the headquarters of the bank, which had practiced modern capitalist financing since 1695. The building now houses the Museum on the Mound, a free exhibit on banking history (see page 57), and is also the Scottish headquarters for Lloyds Banking Group—which swallowed up the Bank of Scotland after the financial crisis of 2008.

If you detour left down Bank Street toward the bank, you'll find the recommended **Whiski Rooms Shop.** If you head in the opposite direction, down George IV Bridge, you'll reach the excellent **National Museum of Scotland,** the famous Greyfriars Bobby statue, restaurant-lined Forrest Road, and photogenic Victoria Street, which leads to the pub-lined Grassmarket square (all described later in this chapter).

Otherwise, continue along the Royal Mile. As you walk, be careful crossing the streets along the Mile. Edinburgh drivers—especially cabbies—have a reputation for being impatient with jaywalking tourists. Notice and heed the pedestrian crossing signals, which don't always turn at the same time as the car signals.

Across the street from Deacon Brodie's Tavern is a seated green statue of hometown boy **David Hume** (1711-1776)—one of the most influential thinkers not only of Scotland, but in all of Western philosophy. The atheistic Hume was one of the towering figures of the Scottish Enlightenment of the mid-1700s. Thinkers and scientists were using the experimental method to challenge and investigate everything, including religion. Hume questioned cause and effect in thought puzzles such as this: We can see that when one billiard ball strikes another, the second one moves, but how do we know the collision "caused" the movement? Notice his shiny toe: People on their way to trial (in the high court just behind the statue) or students on their way to exams (in the nearby university) rub it for good luck.

Follow David Hume's gaze to the opposite corner, where a **brass H** in the pavement marks the site of the last public execution in Edinburgh in 1864. Deacon Brodie himself would have been hung about here (in 1788, on a gallows whose design he had helped to improve—smart guy).

• *From the brass H, continue down the Royal Mile, pausing just before the church square at a stone wellhead with the pyramid cap.*

All along the Royal Mile, **wellheads** like this (from 1835) provided townsfolk with water in the days before buildings had plumbing. This neighborhood well was served by the reservoir up at the castle. Imagine long lines of people in need of water standing here, gossiping and sharing the news. Eventually buildings were retrofitted with water pipes—the ones you see running along building exteriors.

• *Ahead of you (past the Victorian statue of some duke), embedded in the pavement near the street, is a big heart.*

The **Heart of Midlothian** marks the spot of the city's 15th-century municipal building and jail. In times past, in a nearby open space, criminals were hanged, traitors were decapitated, and witches were burned. Citizens hated the rough justice doled out here. Locals still spit on the heart in the pavement. Go ahead...do as the locals do—land one right in the heart of the heart. By the way, Edinburgh has two soccer teams—Heart of Midlothian (known as "Hearts") and Hibernian ("Hibs"). If you're a Hibs fan, spit again.

• *Make your way to the entrance of the church.*

❺ St. Giles' Cathedral

This is the flagship of the Church of Scotland (Scotland's largest denomination)—called the "Mother Church of Presbyterianism." The interior serves as a kind of Scottish Westminster Abbey, filled with monuments, statues, plaques, and

stained-glass windows dedicated to great Scots and moments in history.

A church has stood on this spot since 854, though this structure is an architectural hodgepodge, dating mostly from the 15th through 19th century. In the 16th century, St. Giles' was a kind of national stage on which the drama of the Reformation was played out. The reformer John Knox (1514-1572) was the preacher here. His fiery sermons helped turn once-Catholic Edinburgh into a bastion of Protestantism. During the Scottish Reformation, St. Giles' was transformed from a Catholic cathedral to a Presbyterian church. The spacious interior is well worth a visit, and described in my self-guided tour on page 57.

• *Facing the church entrance, curl around its right side, into a parking lot.*

Sights Around St. Giles'

The grand building across the parking lot from St. Giles' is the **Old Parliament House.** Since the 13th century, the king had ruled a rubber-stamp parliament of nobles and bishops. But the Protestant Reformation promoted democracy, and the parliament gained real power. From the early 1600s until 1707, this building evolved to become the seat of a true parliament of elected officials. That came to an end in 1707, when Scotland signed an Act of Union, joining what's known today as the United Kingdom and giving up their right to self-rule. (More on that later in the walk.) If you're curious to peek inside, head through the door at #11 (free, described on page 61).

The great reformer **John Knox** is buried—with appropriate austerity—under parking lot spot #23. The statue among the cars shows King Charles II riding to a toga party back in 1685.

•*Continue on through the parking lot, around the back end of the church.*

Every Scottish burgh (town licensed by the king to trade) had three standard features: a "tolbooth" (basically a Town Hall, with a courthouse, meeting room, and jail); a "tron" (official weighing scale); and a "mercat" (or market) cross. The **mercat cross** standing just behind St. Giles' Cathedral has a slender column decorated with a unicorn holding a flag with the cross of St. Andrew. Royal proclamations have been read at this mercat cross since the 14th century. In 1952, a town crier heralded the news that Britain had a new queen—three days after the actual event (traditionally the time it took for a horse

to speed here from London). Today, Mercat Cross is the meeting point for many of Edinburgh's walking tours—both historic and ghostly.

• *Circle around to the street side of the church.*

The statue to **Adam Smith** honors the Edinburgh author of the pioneering *Wealth of Nations* (1776), in which he laid out the economics of free-market capitalism. Smith theorized that an "invisible hand" wisely guides the unregulated free market. Stand in front of Smith and imagine the intellectual energy of Edinburgh in the mid-1700s, when it was Europe's most enlightened city. Adam Smith was right in the center of it. He and David Hume were good friends. James Boswell, the famed biographer of Samuel Johnson, took classes from Smith. James Watt, inventor of the steam engine, was another proud Scotsman of the age. With great intellectuals like these, Edinburgh helped create the modern world. The poet Robert Burns, geologist James Hutton (who's considered the father of modern geology), and the publishers of the first *Encyclopedia Britannica* all lived in Edinburgh. Steeped in the inquisitive mindset of the Enlightenment, they applied cool rationality and a secular approach to their respective fields.

• *Head on down the Royal Mile.*

❻ More of High Street

A few steps downhill, at #188 (on the right), is the **Police Information Center.** This place provides a pleasant police presence (say that three times) and a little local law-and-order history to boot. Ask the officer on duty about the impact of modern technology and budget austerity on police work today. Seriously—drop in and discuss whatever law-and-order issue piques your curiosity.

Continuing down this stretch of the Royal Mile, which is traffic-free most of the day (notice the bollards that raise and lower for permitted traffic), you'll see the Fringe Festival office (at #180), street musicians, and another wellhead (with horse "sippies," dating from 1675).

Notice those **three red boxes.** In the 20th century, people used these to make telephone calls to each other. (Imagine that!) These cast-iron booths are produced for all of Britain here in Scotland. As phone booths are decommissioned, some are finding new use as tiny shops, ATMs, and even showing up in residential neighborhoods as nostalgic garden decorations.

At the next intersection, on the left, is **Cockburn Street** (pronounced "COE-burn"). This was cut through High Street's dense wall of medieval skyscrapers in the 1860s to give easy access to the Georgian New Town and the train station. Notice how the sliced buildings were thoughtfully capped with facades that fit the aesthetic look of the Royal Mile. In the Middle Ages, only tiny lanes (like Fleshmarket Close just uphill from Cockburn Street) interrupted the long line of Royal Mile buildings. These days, Cockburn Street has a reputation for its eclectic independent shops and string of trendy bars and eateries.

• *When you reach the* **Tron Church** *(17th century, currently housing shops), you're at the intersection of* **North and South Bridge** *streets. These major streets lead left to Waverley Station and right to the Dalkeith Road B&Bs. Several handy bus lines run along here.*

This is the halfway point of this walk. Stand on the corner diagonally across from the church. Look up to the top of the Royal Mile at the Hub and its 240-foot spire. Notwithstanding its turret and 16th-century charm, the **Radisson Blu Hotel** just across the street is entirely new construction (1990), built to fit in. The city is protecting its historic look. The **Inn on the Mile** next door was once a fancy bank with a lavish interior. As modern banks are moving away from city centers, sumptuous buildings like these are being converted into ornate pubs and restaurants.

In the next block downhill are three **characteristic pubs,** side by side, that offer free traditional Scottish and folk music in the evenings. Notice the chimneys. Tenement buildings shared stairways and entries, but held individual apartments, each with its own chimney. Take a look back at the spire of St. Giles' Cathedral—inspired by the Scottish crown and the thistle, Scotland's national flower.

• *Go down High Street another block, passing near the* **Museum of Childhood** *(on the right, at #42, and worth a stop; see page 62) and a fragrant* **fudge shop** *a few doors down, where you can sample various flavors (tempting you to buy a slab).*

Directly across the street, just below another wellhead, is the...

❼ John Knox House

Remember that Knox was a towering figure in Edinburgh's history, converting Scotland to a Calvinist style of Protestantism. His religious bent was "Presbyterianism," in which parishes are governed by elected officials rather than appointed bishops. This more democratic brand of Christianity also spurred Scotland toward political democracy. If you're interested in Knox or the Reformation, this sight is worth a visit (see page 62). Full disclosure: It's not certain that Knox ever actually lived here. Attached to the Knox House is the Scottish Storytelling Centre, where locals with the gift of gab perform regularly; check the posted schedule.

• *A few steps farther down High Street, at the intersection with St. Mary's and Jeffrey streets, you'll reach...*

❽ The World's End

For centuries, a wall stood here, marking the end of the burgh of

Edinburgh. For residents within the protective walls of the city, this must have felt like the "world's end," indeed. The area beyond was called Canongate, a monastic community associated with Holyrood Abbey. At the intersection, find the brass bricks in the street that trace the gate (demolished in 1764). Look to the right down St. Mary's Street about 200 yards to see a surviving bit of that old wall, known as the **Flodden Wall.** In the 1513 Battle of Flodden, the Scottish king James IV made the disastrous decision to invade northern England. James and 10,000 of his Scotsmen were killed. Fearing a brutal English counterattack, Edinburgh scrambled to reinforce its broken-down city wall. To the left, down Jeffrey Street, you'll see Scotland's top tattoo parlor, and a supplier for a different kind of tattoo (the Scottish Regimental Store).

• *Continue down the Royal Mile—leaving old Edinburgh—as High Street changes names to...*

❾ Canongate

About 10 steps down Canongate, look left down Cranston Street (past the train tracks) to a good view of the Calton Cemetery up on **Calton Hill.** The obelisk, called Martyrs' Monument, remembers a group of 18th-century patriots exiled by London to Australia for their reform politics. The round building to the left is the grave of philosopher David Hume. And the big, turreted building to the

right was the jail master's house. Today, the main reason to go up Calton Hill is for the fine views (described on page 85).

The giant, blocky building that dominates the lower slope of the hill is **St. Andrew's House,** headquarters of the Scottish Government—including the office of the first minister of Scotland. According to locals, the building has also been an important base for MI6, Britain's version of the CIA. Wait a minute—isn't James Bond Scottish? Hmmm...

• *A couple hundred yards farther along the Royal Mile (on the right at #172) you reach* **Cadenhead's,** *a serious place to learn about and buy whisky (see page 89). About 30 yards farther along, you'll pass two worthwhile and free museums, the* **People's Story Museum** *(on the left, in the old tollhouse at #163) and the Museum of Edinburgh (on the right,* *at #142; for more on both, see page 63). But our next stop is the church just across from the* **Museum of Edinburgh.**

The 1688 **Canongate Kirk** (Church)—located not far from the royal residence of Holyroodhouse—is where Queen Elizabeth II and her family worship when-

ever they're in town. (So don't sit in the front pew, marked with her crown.) The gilded emblem at the top of the roof, high above the door, has the antlers of a stag from the royal estate of Balmoral. The Queen's granddaughter married here in 2011.

The church is open only when volunteers have signed up to welcome visitors (and closed in winter). Chat them up and borrow the description of the place. Then step inside the lofty blue and red interior, renovated with royal money; the church is filled with light and the flags of various Scottish regiments. In the narthex, peruse the photos of royal family events here, and find the list of priests and ministers of this parish—it goes back to 1143 (with a clear break with the Reformation in 1561).

Outside, turn right as you leave the church and walk up into the graveyard. The large, gated grave (abutting the back of the People's Story Museum) is the affectionately tended tomb of **Adam Smith,** the father of capitalism. (Throw him a penny or two.)

Just outside the churchyard, the statue on the sidewalk is of the poet **Robert Fergusson.** One of the first to write verse in the Scots language, he so inspired Robert Burns that Burns paid for Fergusson's tombstone in the Canongate churchyard and composed his epitaph.

Now look across the street at the **gabled house** next to the Museum of Edinburgh. Scan the facade to see shells put there in the 17th century to defend against the evil power of witches yet to be drowned.

• *Walk about 300 yards farther along. In the distance you can see the Palace of Holyroodhouse (the end of this walk) and soon, on the right, you'll come to the modern Scottish parliament building.*

Just opposite the parliament building is **White Horse Close** (on the left, in the white arcade). Step into this 17th-century courtyard. It was from here that the Edinburgh stagecoach left for London. Eight days later, the horse-drawn carriage would pull into its destination: Scotland Yard. Note that bus #35 leaves

in two directions from here—downhill for the Royal Yacht *Britannia,* and uphill along the Royal Mile (as far as South Bridge) and on to the National Museum of Scotland.

• *Now walk up around the corner to the flagpoles (flying the flags of Europe, Britain, and Scotland) in front of the...*

❿ Scottish Parliament Building

Finally, after centuries of history, we reach the 21st century. And finally, after three centuries of London rule, Scotland has a parliament building...in Scotland.

When Scotland united with England in 1707, its parliament was dissolved. But in 1999, the Scottish parliament was reestablished, and in 2004, it moved into this striking new home. Notice how the eco-friendly building, by the Catalan architect Enric Miralles, mixes wild angles, lots of light, bold windows, oak, and native stone into a startling complex. (People from Catalunya—another would-be breakaway nation—have an affinity for Scotland.) From the front of the parliament building, look in the distance at the rocky Salisbury Crags, with people hiking the traverse up to the dramatic next summit called Arthur's Seat. Now look at the building in relation to the craggy cliffs. The architect envisioned the building as if it were rising right from the base of Arthur's Seat, almost bursting from the rock.

Since it celebrates Scottish democracy, the architecture is not a statement of authority. There are no statues of old heroes. There's not even a grand entry. You feel like you're entering an office park. Given its neighborhood, the media often calls the Scottish Parliament "Holyrood" for short (similar to calling the US Congress "Capitol Hill"). For details on touring the building and seeing parliament in action, see page 64.

• *Across the street is the **Queen's Gallery**, where she shares part of her amazing personal art collection in excellent revolving exhibits (see page 66). Finally, walk to the end of the road (Abbey Strand), and step up to the impressive wrought-iron gate of the Queen's palace. Look up at the stag with its holy cross, or "holy rood," on its forehead, and peer into the palace grounds. (The ticket office and palace entryway, a fine café, and a handy WC are just through the arch on the right.)*

⓫ Palace of Holyroodhouse

Since the 16th century, this palace has marked the end of the Royal Mile. An abbey—part of a 12th-century Augustinian monastery—originally stood in its place. While most of that old building is

gone, you can see the surviving nave behind the palace on the left. According to one legend, it was named "holy rood" for a piece of the cross, brought here as a relic by Queen (and later Saint) Margaret. (Another version of the story is that King David I, Margaret's son, saw the image of a cross upon a stag's head while hunting here and took it as a sign that he should build an abbey on the site.) Because Scotland's royalty preferred living at Holyroodhouse to the blustery castle on the rock, the palace grew over time. If the Queen's not visiting, the palace welcomes visitors (see page 65 for details).

• *Your walk—from the castle to the palace, with so much Scottish history packed in between—is complete. And, if your appetite is whetted for more, don't worry; you've just scratched the surface. Enjoy the rest of Edinburgh.*

BONNIE WEE NEW TOWN WALK

Many visitors, mesmerized by the Royal Mile, never venture to the New Town. And that's a shame. With some of the city's finest Georgian architecture (from its 18th-century boom period), the New Town has a completely different character than the Old Town. This self-guided walk—worth ▲▲—gives you a quick orientation in about one hour.

• *Begin on Waverley Bridge, spanning the gully between the Old and New towns; to get there from the Royal Mile, just head down the curved Cockburn Street near the Tron Church (or cut down any of the "close" lanes opposite St. Giles' Cathedral). Stand on the bridge overlooking the train tracks, facing the castle.*

View from Waverley Bridge: From this vantage point, you can enjoy fine views of medieval Edinburgh, with its 10-story-plus "skyscrapers." It's easy to imagine how miserably crowded this area was, prompting the expansion of the city during the Georgian period. Pick out landmarks along the Royal Mile, most notably the open-work steeple of St. Giles'.

A big lake called the **Nor' Loch** once was to the north (nor') of the Old Town; now it's a valley between Edinburgh's two towns. The lake was drained around 1800 as part of the expansion. Before that, the lake was the town's water reservoir...and its sewer. Much has been written about the town's infamous stink (a.k.a. the "flowers of Edinburgh"). The town's nickname, "Auld Reekie," referred to both the smoke of its industry and the stench of its squalor.

The long-gone loch was also a handy place for drowning witches. With their thumbs tied to their ankles, they'd be lashed to dunking stools. Those who survived the ordeal were considered "aided by the devil" and burned as witches. If they died, they were innocent and given a good Christian burial. Edinburgh was Europe's witch-burning mecca—any perceived "sign," including a small birthmark, could condemn you. Scotland burned more witches per capita than any other country—17,000 souls between 1479 and 1722.

Visually trace the train tracks as they disappear into a tunnel below the **Scottish National Gallery** (with lesser-known paintings by great European artists; you can visit it during this walk—see page 71). The two fine Neoclassical buildings of the National Gallery date from the 1840s and sit upon a mound that's called, well, **The Mound.** When the New Town was built, tons of rubble from the excavations were piled here

(1781-1830), forming a dirt bridge that connected the new development with the Old Town to allay merchant concerns about being cut off from the future heart of the city.

Turning 180 degrees (and facing the ramps down into the train station), notice the huge, turreted building with the clock tower. **The Balmoral** was one of the city's two grand hotels during its glory days (its opposite bookend, the **Waldorf Astoria Edinburgh,** sits at the far end of the former lakebed—near the end of this walk). Aristocrats arriving by train could use a hidden entrance to go from the platform directly up to their plush digs. (Today The Balmoral is known mostly as the place where J. K. Rowling completed the final Harry Potter book.)

• *Now walk across the bridge toward the New Town. Before the corner, enter the gated gardens on the left, and head toward the big, pointy monument. You're at the edge of...*

❶ **Princes Street Gardens:** This grassy park, filling the former lakebed, offers a wonderful escape from the bustle of the city. Once the private domain of the wealthy, it was opened to the public around 1870—not as a democratic gesture, but in hopes of increas-

Bonnie Wee New Town Walk

① Princes Street Gardens
② Scott Monument
③ Jenners Department Store
④ St. Andrew Square
⑤ George Street
⑥ St. Andrew's & St. George's Church
⑦ The Dome Restaurant
⑧ King George IV Statue
⑨ Thistle Street
⑩ William Pitt Statue
⑪ Rose Street
⑫ Charlotte Square
⑬ Georgian House

ing sales at the Princes Street department stores. Join the office workers for a picnic lunch break.

• *Take a seat on the bench indicated by the Livingstone (Dr. Livingstone, I presume?) statue. (The Victorian explorer is well equipped with a guidebook, but is hardly packing light—his lion skin doesn't even fit in his rucksack carry-on.)*

Look up at the towering...

❷ **Scott Monument:** Built in the early 1840s, this elaborate Neo-Gothic monument honors the great author Sir Walter Scott, one of Edinburgh's many illustrious sons. When Scott died in 1832, it was said that "Scotland never owed so much to one man." Scott almost singlehandedly created the Scotland we know. Just as the country was in danger of being assimilated into England, Scott celebrated traditional songs, legends, myths, architecture, and kilts, thereby reviving the Highland culture and cementing a national identity. And, as the father of the Romantic historical novel, he contributed to Western literature in general. The 200-foot monument shelters a marble statue of Scott and his favorite pet, Maida, a deerhound who was one of 30 canines this dog lover owned during his lifetime. They're sur-

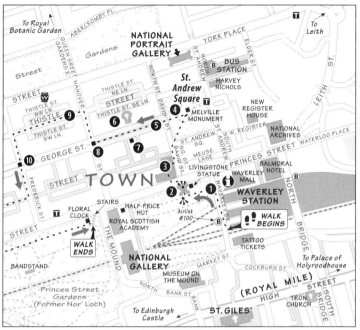

rounded by busts of 16 great Scottish poets and 64 characters from his books. Climbing the tight, stony spiral staircase of 287 steps earns you a peek at a tiny museum midway, a fine city view at the top, and intimate encounters going up and down (£5, daily 10:00-19:00, Oct-March until 16:00, tel. 0131/529-4068). For more on Scott, see page 60.

• *Exit the gate near Livingstone and head across busy Princes Street to the venerable...*

❸ **Jenners Department Store:** As you wait for the light to change (and wait...and wait...), notice how statues of women sup-

port the building—just as real women support the business. The arrival of new fashions here was such a big deal in the old days that they'd announce it by flying flags on the Nelson Monument atop Calton Hill.

Step inside and head upstairs into the grand, skylit atrium. The central space—filled with a towering tree at Christmas—is classic Industrial Age architecture. The Queen's coat of arms high on the wall indicates she shops here.

• *From the atrium, turn right and exit onto South St. David Street. Turn left and follow this street uphill one block up to...*

❹ St. Andrew Square: This green space is dedicated to the patron saint of Scotland. In the early 19th century, there were no shops around here—just fine residences; this was a private garden for the fancy people living here. Now open to the public, the square is a popular lunch hangout for workers. The Melville Monument honors a powermonger member of parliament who, for four decades (around 1800), was nicknamed the "uncrowned king of Scotland."

One block up from the top of the park is the excellent **Scottish National Portrait Gallery,** which introduces you to all of the biggest names in Scottish history (described later, under "Sights in Edinburgh").

• *Follow the Melville Monument's gaze straight ahead out of the park. Cross the street and stand at the top of...*

❺ George Street: This is the main drag of Edinburgh's grid-planned New Town. Laid out in 1776, when King George III was busy putting down a revolution in a troublesome overseas colony, the New Town was a model of urban planning in its day. The architectural style is "Georgian"—British for "Neoclassical." And the street plan came with an unambiguous message: to celebrate the union of Scotland with England into the United Kingdom. (This was particularly important, since Scotland was just two decades removed from the failed Jacobite uprising of Bonnie Prince Charlie.)

St. Andrew Square (patron saint of Scotland) and Charlotte Square (George III's queen) bookend the New Town, with its three main streets named for the royal family of the time (George, Queen, and Princes). Thistle and Rose streets—which we'll see near the end of this walk—are named for the national flowers of Scotland and England.

The plan for the New Town was the masterstroke of the 23-year-old urban designer James Craig. George Street—20 feet wider than the others (so a four-horse carriage could make a U-turn)—was the main drag. Running down the high spine of the area, it afforded grand, unobstructed views (thanks to the parks on either side) of the River Forth in one direction and the Old Town in the other. As you stroll down the street, you'll notice that Craig's grid is a series of axes designed to connect monuments new and old; later architects made certain to continue this harmony. For example, notice that the Scott Monument lines up perfectly with this first intersection.

• *Halfway down the first block of George Street, on the right, is...*

❻ St. Andrew's and St. George's Church: Designed as part of the New Town plan in the 1780s, the church is a product of the Scottish Enlightenment. It has an elliptical plan (the first in Britain) so that all can focus on the pulpit. If it's open, step inside. A fine leaflet tells the story of the church, and a handy cafeteria downstairs serves cheap and cheery lunches.

Directly across the street from the church is another temple, this one devoted to money. This former bank building (now housing the recommended restaurant ❼ **The Dome**) has a pediment filled with figures demonstrating various ways to make money, which they do with all the nobility of classical gods. Consider scurrying across the street and ducking inside to view the stunning domed atrium.

Continue down George Street to the intersection with a ❽ statue commemorating the visit by **King George IV.** Notice the particularly fine axis formed by this cross-street: The National Gallery lines up perfectly with the Royal Mile's skyscrapers and the former Tolbooth Church, creating a Gotham City collage.

• *By now you've gotten your New Town bearings. Feel free to stop this walk here: If you were to turn left and head down Hanover Street, in a block you'd run into the Scottish National Gallery; the street behind it curves back up to the Royal Mile.*

But to see more of the New Town—including the Georgian House, offering an insightful look inside one of these fine 18th-century homes— stick with me for a few more long blocks, zigzagging through side streets to see the various personalities that inhabit this rigid grid.

Turn right on Hanover Street; after just one (short) block, cross over and go down...

❾ **Thistle Street:** Of the many streets in the New Town, this has perhaps the most vivid Scottish character. And that's fitting, as it's named after Scotland's national flower. At the beginning and end of the street, also notice that Craig's street plan included tranquil cul-de-sacs within the larger blocks. Thistle Street seems sleepy, but holds characteristic boutiques and good restaurants (see "Eating in Edinburgh," later). Halfway down the street on the left, Howie Nicholsby's shop, 21st Century Kilt, updates traditional Scottish menswear.

You'll pop out at Frederick Street. Turning left, you'll see a ❿ statue of **William Pitt,** prime minister under King George III. (Pitt's father gave his name to the American city of Pittsburgh— which Scots pronounce as "Pitts-burrah"...I assume.)

• *For an interesting contrast, we'll continue down another side street.*

Pass the statue of Pitt (heading toward Edinburgh Castle), and turn right onto...

⓫ Rose Street: As a rose is to a thistle, and as England is to Scotland, so is brash, boisterous Rose Street to sedate, thoughtful

Thistle Street. This stretch of Rose Street feels more commercialized, jammed with chain stores; the second block is packed with pubs and restaurants. As you walk, keep an eye out for the cobbled Tudor rose embedded in the brick sidewalk. When you cross the aptly named Castle Street, linger over the grand views to Edinburgh Castle. It's almost as if they planned it this way...just for the views.

• *Popping out at the far end of Rose Street, across the street and to your right is...*

⓬ Charlotte Square: The building of the New Town started cheap with St. Andrew Square, but finished well with this stately

space. In 1791, the Edinburgh town council asked the prestigious Scottish architect Robert Adam to pump up the design for Charlotte Square. The council hoped that Adam's plan would answer criticism that the New Town buildings lacked innovation or ambition— and they got what they wanted. Adam's design, which raised the standard of New Town architecture to "international class," created Edinburgh's finest Georgian square.

• *Along the right side of Charlotte Square, at #7 (just left of the pointy pediment), you can visit the* **⓭ Georgian House,** *which gives you a great peek behind all of these harmonious Neoclassical facades (see page 79).*

When you're done touring the house, you can head back through the New Town grid, perhaps taking some different streets than the way you came. Or, for a restful return to our starting point, consider this...

Return Through Princes Street Gardens: From Charlotte Square, drop down to busy Princes Street (noticing the red building to the right—the grand Waldorf Astoria Hotel and twin sister of The Balmoral at the start of our walk). But rather than walking along the busy bus-and-tram-lined shopping drag, head into **Princes Street Gardens** (cross Princes Street and enter the gate on the left). With the castle looming overhead, you'll pass a playground, a fanciful Victorian fountain, more monuments to great Scots, war memorials, and a bandstand (which hosts Scottish country dancing—see page 95—as well as occasional big-name acts). Finally you'll reach a staircase up to the Scottish National Gallery; notice the oldest **floral clock** in the world on your left as you climb up.

• *Our walk is over. From here, you can tour the gallery; head up Bank Street just behind it to reach the Royal Mile; hop on a bus along Princes Street to your next stop (or B&B); or continue through another stretch of the Princes Street Gardens to the Scott Monument and our starting point.*

Sights in Edinburgh

▲▲▲EDINBURGH CASTLE

The fortified birthplace of the city 1,300 years ago, this imposing symbol of Edinburgh sits proudly on a rock high above you. The home of Scotland's kings and queens for centuries, the castle has witnessed royal births, medieval pageantry, and bloody sieges. Today it's a complex of various buildings, the oldest dating from the 12th century, linked by cobbled roads that survive from its more recent use  as a military garrison. The castle—with expansive views, plenty of history, and the stunning crown jewels of Scotland—is a fascinating and multifaceted sight that deserves several hours of your time.

Cost and Hours: £17, daily 9:30-18:00, Oct-March until 17:00, last entry one hour before closing, tel. 0131/225-9846, www.edinburghcastle.gov.uk.

Avoiding Lines: The castle is usually less crowded after 14:00 or so; if planning a morning visit, the earlier the better. To avoid ticket lines (worst in Aug), book online and print your ticket at home. You can also pick up your prebooked ticket at machines just inside the entrance or at the visitor information desk a few steps uphill on the right. You can also skip the ticket line with a Historic Scotland Explorer Pass.

Getting There: Simply walk up the Royal Mile (if arriving by bus from the B&B area south of the city, get off at South Bridge and huff up the Mile for about 15 minutes). Taxis get you closer, dropping you a block below the esplanade at the Hub/Tolbooth Church.

Tours: Thirty-minute introductory **guided tours** are free with admission (2-4/hour, depart from Argyle Battery, see clock for next departure; fewer off-season). The informative **audioguide** provides four hours of descriptions, including the National War Museum Scotland (£3 if you purchase with your ticket; £3.50 if you rent it once inside, pick up inside Portcullis Gate).

Eating: You have two choices within the castle. The **$ Redcoat Café**—just past the Argyle Battery—is a big, bright, efficient cafeteria with great views. The **$$ Tea Rooms** in Crown Square serves sit-down meals and afternoon tea. A whisky shop, with tastings, is just through Foog's Gate.

⊙ Self-Guided Tour

From the ❶ **entry gate,** start winding your way uphill toward the main sights— the crown jewels and the Royal Palace—located near the summit. Since the castle was protected on three sides by sheer cliffs, the main defense had to be here at the entrance. During the castle's heyday in the 1500s, a 100-foot tower loomed overhead, facing the city.

• *Passing through the portcullis gate, you reach the...*

❷ **Argyle (Six-Gun) Battery, with View:** These front-loading, cast-iron cannons are from the Napoleonic era (c. 1800), when the castle was still a force to be reckoned with.

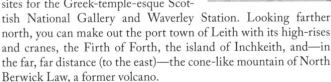

From here, look north across the valley to the grid of the New Town. The valley sits where the Nor' Loch once was; this lake was drained and filled in when the New Town was built in the late 1700s, its swamps replaced with gardens. Later the land provided sites for the Greek-temple-esque Scottish National Gallery and Waverley Station. Looking farther north, you can make out the port town of Leith with its high-rises and cranes, the Firth of Forth, the island of Inchkeith, and—in the far, far distance (to the east)—the cone-like mountain of North Berwick Law, a former volcano.

Now look down. The sheer north precipice looks impregnable.

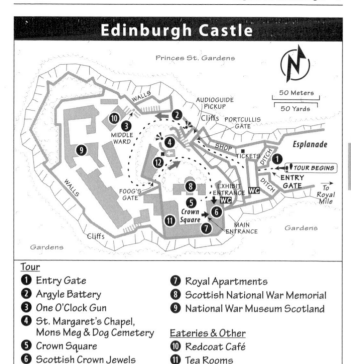

Edinburgh Castle

Princes St. Gardens

AUDIOGUIDE PICKUP

Cliffs PORTCULLIS GATE

50 Meters
50 Yards

WALLS

MIDDLE WARD

Esplanade

SHOP

TICKETS

DITCH

TOUR BEGINS

ENTRY GATE

WALLS

FOOG'S GATE

EXHIBIT ENTRANCE WC

WC

To Royal Mile

Crown Square

MAIN ENTRANCE

Gardens

Cliffs

Gardens

EDINBURGH

Tour
❶ Entry Gate
❷ Argyle Battery
❸ One O'Clock Gun
❹ St. Margaret's Chapel, Mons Meg & Dog Cemetery
❺ Crown Square
❻ Scottish Crown Jewels (Honours of Scotland)
❼ Royal Apartments
❽ Scottish National War Memorial
❾ National War Museum Scotland

Eateries & Other
❿ Redcoat Café
⓫ Tea Rooms
⓬ Whisky Shop

But on the night of March 14, 1314, 30 armed men silently scaled this rock face. They were loyal to Robert the Bruce and determined to recapture the castle, which had fallen into English hands. They caught the English by surprise, took the castle, and—three months later—Bruce defeated the English at the Battle of Bannockburn.

· *A little farther along, near the café, is the...*

❸ **One O'Clock Gun:** Crowds gather for the 13:00 gun blast, a tradition that gives ships in the bay something to set their navigational devices by. Before the gun, sailors set their clocks with help from the Nelson Monument—that's the tall pillar in the distance on Calton Hill. The monument has a "time ball" affixed to the cross on top, which drops precisely at the top of the hour. But on foggy days, ships couldn't see the ball, so the cannon shot was instituted instead (1861). The tradition stuck, every day at 13:00. (Locals joke that the frugal Scots don't fire it at high noon, as that would cost 11 extra rounds a day.)

· *Continue uphill, winding to the left and passing through Foog's Gate. At the very top of the hill, on your left, is...*

❹ **St. Margaret's Chapel:** This tiny stone chapel is Edinburgh's oldest building (around 1120) and sits atop its highest point

(440 feet). It represents the birth of the city.

In 1057, Malcolm III murdered King Macbeth (of Shakespeare fame) and assumed the Scottish throne. Later, he married Princess Margaret, and the family settled atop this hill. Their marriage united Malcolm's Highland Scots with Margaret's Lowland Anglo-Saxons—the cultural mix that would define Edinburgh.

Step inside the tiny, unadorned church—a testament to Margaret's reputed piety. The style is Romanesque. The nave is wonderfully simple, with classic Norman zigzags decorating the round arch that separates the tiny nave from the sacristy. You'll see a facsimile of St. Margaret's 11th-century gospel book. The small (modern) stained-glass windows feature St. Margaret herself, St. Columba, and St. Ninian (who brought Christianity to Scotland in A.D. 397), St. Andrew (Scotland's patron saint), and William Wallace (the defender of Scotland). These days, the place is popular for weddings. (As it seats only 20, it's particularly popular with brides' parents.)

Margaret died at the castle in 1093, and her son King David I built this chapel in her honor (she was sainted in 1250). David

expanded the castle and also founded Holyrood Abbey, across town. These two structures were soon linked by a Royal Mile of buildings, and Edinburgh was born.

Mons Meg, in front of the church, is a huge and once-upon-a-time frightening 15th-century siege cannon that fired 330-pound stones nearly two miles. Imagine. It was a gift from Philip the Good, duke of Burgundy, to his great-niece's husband King James II of Scotland.

Nearby, belly up to the banister and look down to find the **Dog Cemetery,** a tiny patch of grass with a sweet little line of doggie tombstones, marking the graves of soldiers' faithful canines in arms.

• *Continue on, curving downhill into...*

❺ **Crown Square:** This courtyard is the center of today's Royal Castle complex. Get oriented. You're surrounded by the crown jewels, the

Royal Palace (with its Great Hall), and the Scottish National War Memorial.

The castle has evolved over the centuries, and Crown Square is relatively "new." After the time of Malcolm and Margaret, the castle was greatly expanded by David II (1324-1371), complete with tall towers, a Great Hall, dungeon, cellars, and so on. This served as the grand royal residence for two centuries. Then, in 1571-1573, the Protestant citizens of Edinburgh laid siege to the castle and its Catholic/monarchist holdouts, eventually blasting it to smithereens. (You can tour the paltry remains of the medieval castle in nearby **David's Tower.**) The palace was rebuilt nearby—around what is today's Crown Square.

• We'll tour the buildings around Crown Square. First up: the crown jewels. Look for two entrances. The one on Crown Square, only open in peak season, deposits you straight into the room with the crown jewels but usually comes with a line. The other entry, around the side (near the WCs), takes you—often at a shuffle—through the interesting, Disney-esque "Honours of Scotland" exhibition, which tells the story of the crown jewels and how they survived the harrowing centuries, but lacks any actual artifacts.

❻ Scottish Crown Jewels (Honours of Scotland): For centuries, Scotland's monarchs were crowned in elaborate rituals involving three wondrous objects: a jewel-studded crown, scepter, and sword. These objects—along with the ceremonial Stone of Scone (pronounced "skoon")—are known as the "Honours of Scotland." Scotland's crown jewels may not be as impressive as England's, but they're treasured by locals as a symbol of Scottish nationalism. They're also older than England's; while Oliver Cromwell destroyed England's jewels, the Scots managed to hide theirs.

History of the Jewels: The Honours of Scotland exhibit that leads up to the Crown Room traces the evolution of the jewels, the ceremony, and the often-turbulent journey of this precious regalia. Here's the SparkNotes version:

In 1306, Robert the Bruce was crowned with a "circlet of gold" in a ceremony at Scone—a town 40 miles north of Edinburgh, which Scotland's earliest kings had claimed as their capital. Around 1500, King James IV added two new items to the coronation ceremony—a scepter (a gift from the pope) and a huge sword (a gift from another pope). In 1540, James V had the original crown aug-

mented by an Edinburgh goldsmith, giving it the imperial-crown shape it has today.

William Wallace (c. 1270-1305)

In 1286, Scotland's king died without an heir, plunging the prosperous country into a generation of chaos. As Scottish nobles bickered over naming a successor, the English King Edward I—nicknamed "Longshanks" because of his long legs—invaded and assumed power (1296). He placed a figurehead on the throne, forced Scottish nobles to sign a pledge of allegiance to England (the "Ragman's Roll"), moved the British parliament north to York, and took the highly symbolic Stone of Scone to London, where it would remain for centuries.

WILLIAM WALLACE.

A year later, the Scots rose up against Edward, led by William Wallace (popularized in the film *Braveheart*). A mix of history and legend portrays Wallace as the son of a poor-but-knightly family that refused to sign the Ragman's Roll. Exceptionally tall and strong, he learned Latin and French from two uncles, who were priests. In his teenage years, his father and older brother were killed by the English. Later, he killed an English sheriff to avenge the death of his wife, Marion. Wallace's rage inspired his fellow Scots to revolt.

In the summer of 1297, Wallace and his guerrillas scored a series of stunning victories over the English. On September 11, a well-equipped English army of 10,000 soldiers and 300 horsemen began crossing Stirling Bridge. Wallace's men attacked, and in the chaos, the bridge collapsed, splitting the English ranks in two. The ragtag Scots drove the confused English into the river. The Battle of Stirling Bridge was a rout, and Wallace was knighted and appointed guardian of Scotland.

All through the winter, King Edward's men chased Wallace, continually frustrated by the Scots' hit-and-run tactics. Finally, at the Battle of Falkirk (1298), they drew Wallace's men out onto the open battlefield. The English with their horses and archers easily destroyed the spear-carrying Scots. Wallace resigned in disgrace and went on the lam, while his successors negotiated truces with the English, finally surrendering unconditionally in 1304. Wallace alone held out.

In 1305, the English tracked him down and took him to London, where he was convicted of treason and mocked with a crown of oak leaves as the "king of outlaws." On August 23, they stripped him naked and dragged him to the execution site. There he was strangled to near death, castrated, and dismembered. His head was stuck on a spike atop London Bridge, while his body parts were sent on tour to spook would-be rebels. But Wallace's martyrdom only served to inspire his countrymen, and the torch of independence was picked up by Robert the Bruce (see page 54). Despite the *Braveheart* movie, Robert the Bruce, not Wallace, was considered the original "Braveheart."

These Honours were used to crown every monarch: nine-month-old Mary, Queen of Scots (she cried); her one-year-old son James VI (future king of England); and Charles I and II. But the days of divine-right rulers were numbered.

In 1649, the parliament had Charles I (king of both England and Scotland) beheaded. Soon Cromwell's rabid English antiroyalists were marching on Edinburgh. Quick! Legend says two women scooped up the crown and sword, hid them in their skirts and belongings, and buried them in a church far to the northeast until the coast was clear.

When the monarchy was restored, the regalia were used to crown Scotland's last king, Charles II (1660). Then, in 1707, the Treaty of Union with England ended Scotland's independence. The Honours came out for a ceremony to bless the treaty, and were then locked away in a strongbox in the castle. There they lay for over a century, until Sir Walter Scott—the writer and great champion of Scottish tradition—forced a detailed search of the castle in 1818. The box was found...and there the Honours were, perfectly preserved. Within a few years, they were put on display, as they have been ever since.

The crown's most recent official appearance was in 1999, when it was taken across town to the grand opening of the reinstated parliament, marking a new chapter in the Scottish nation. As it represents the monarchy, the crown is present whenever a new session of parliament opens. (And if Scotland ever secedes, you can be sure that crown will be in the front row.)

The Honours: Finally, you enter the Crown Room to see the regalia itself. The four-foot steel **sword** was made in Italy under orders of Pope Julius II (the man who also commissioned Michelangelo's Sistine Chapel and St. Peter's Basilica). The **scepter** is made of silver, covered with gold, and topped with a rock crystal and a pearl. The gem- and pearl-encrusted **crown** has an imperial arch topped with a cross. Legend says the band of gold in the center is the original crown that once adorned the head of Robert the Bruce.

The **Stone of Scone** (a.k.a. the "Stone of Destiny") sits plain and strong next to the jewels. It's a rough-hewn gray slab of sandstone, about 26 by 17 by 10 inches. As far back as the ninth century, Scotland's kings were crowned atop this stone, when it stood at the medieval capital of Scone. But in 1296, the invading army of Edward I of England carried the stone off to Westminster Abbey. For the next seven centuries, English (and subsequently British) kings and queens were crowned sitting on a coronation chair with the Stone of Scone tucked in a compartment underneath.

In 1950, four Scottish students broke into Westminster Abbey on Christmas Day and smuggled the stone back to Scotland in an act of foolhardy patriotism. But what could they do with it? After three months, they abandoned the stone, draped in Scotland's national flag. It was returned to Westminster Abbey, where (in 1953) Queen Elizabeth II was crowned atop it. In 1996, in recognition of increased Scottish autonomy, Elizabeth agreed to let the stone go home, on one condition: that it be returned to Westminster Abbey for all British coronations. One day, the next monarch of the United Kingdom—Prince Charles is first in line—will sit atop it, re-enacting a coronation ritual that dates back a thousand years.

• *Exit the crown jewel display, heading down the stairs. But just before exiting into the courtyard, turn left through a door that leads into the...*

❼ **Royal Apartments:** Scottish royalty lived in the Royal Palace only when safety or protocol required it (they preferred the Palace of Holyroodhouse at the bottom of the Royal Mile). Here you can see several historic but unimpressive rooms. The first one, labeled **Queen Mary's Chamber,** is where Mary, Queen of Scots (1542-1587), gave birth to James VI of Scotland, who later became King James I of England. Nearby **Laich Hall** (Lower Hall) was the dining room of the royal family.

The **Great Hall** (through a separate entrance on Crown Square) was built by James IV to host the castle's official banquets and meetings. It's still used for such purposes today. Most of the

interior—its fireplace, carved walls, pikes, and armor—is Victorian. But the well-constructed wood ceiling is original. This hammer-beam roof (constructed like the hull of a ship) is self-supporting. The complex system of braces and arches distributes the weight of the roof outward to the walls, so there's no need for supporting pillars or long cross beams. Before leaving, look for the big iron-barred peephole above the fireplace, on the right. This allowed the king to spy on his subjects while they partied.

• *Across the Crown Square courtyard is the...*

❽ **Scottish National War Memorial:** This commemorates the 149,000 Scottish soldiers lost in World War I, the 58,000

who died in World War II, and the nearly 800 (and counting) lost in British battles since. This is a somber spot (stow your camera and phone). Paid for by public donations, each bay is dedicated to a particular Scottish regiment. The main shrine, featuring a green Italian-marble memorial that contains the original WWI rolls of honor, sits on an exposed chunk of the castle rock. Above you, the archangel Michael is busy slaying a dragon. The bronze frieze accurately shows the attire of various wings of Scotland's military. The stained glass starts with Cain and Abel on the left, and finishes with a celebration of peace on the right. To appreciate how important this place is, consider that Scottish soldiers died at twice the rate of other British soldiers in World War I.

• *Our final stop is worth the five-minute walk to get there. Backtrack to the café (and One O'Clock Gun), then head downhill to the War Museum. The statue in the courtyard in front of the museum is* **Field Marshall Sir Douglas Haig**—*the Scotsman who commanded the British Army through the WWI trench warfare of the Battle of the Somme and in Flanders Fields.*

❾ National War Museum Scotland: This thoughtful museum covers four centuries of Scottish military history. Instead of the usual musty, dusty displays of endless armor, there's a compelling mix of videos, uniforms, weapons, medals, mementos, and eloquent excerpts from soldiers' letters.

Here you'll learn the story of how the fierce and courageous Scottish warrior changed from being a symbol of resistance against Britain to being a champion of that same empire. Along the way, these military men received many decorations for valor and did more than their share of dying in battle. But even when fighting alongside—rather than against—England, Scottish regiments still promoted their romantic, kilted-warrior image.

Queen Victoria fueled this ideal throughout the 19th century. She was infatuated with the Scottish Highlands and the culture's untamed, rustic mystique. Highland soldiers, especially officers, went to great personal expense to sport all their elaborate regalia, and the kilted men fought best to the tune of their beloved bagpipes. For centuries the stirring drone of bagpipes accompanied Highland soldiers into battle—raising their spirits and announcing to the enemy that they were about to meet a fierce and mighty foe.

This museum shows the human side of war as well as the clev-

EDINBURGH

Robert the Bruce (1274-1329)

In 1314, Robert the Bruce's men attacked Edinburgh's Royal Castle, recapturing it from the English. It was just one of many intense battles between the oppressive English and the plucky Scots during the Wars of Independence.

In this era, Scotland had to overcome not only its English foes but also its own divisiveness—and no one was more divided than Robert the Bruce. As earl of Carrick, he was born with blood ties to England and a long-standing family claim to the Scottish throne.

When England's King Edward I ("Longshanks") conquered Scotland in 1296, the Bruce family welcomed it, hoping Edward would defeat their rivals and put Bruce's father on the throne. They dutifully signed the "Ragman's Roll" of allegiance—and then Edward chose someone else as king.

Twentysomething Robert the Bruce (the "the" comes from his original family name of "de Bruce") then joined William Wallace's revolt against the English. As legend has it, he was the one who knighted Wallace after the victory at Stirling Bridge. When Wallace fell from favor, Bruce became a guardian of Scotland (caretaker ruler in the absence of a king) and continued fighting the English. But when Edward's armies again got the upper hand in 1302, Robert—along with Scotland's other nobles—diplomatically surrendered and again pledged loyalty.

In 1306, Robert the Bruce murdered his chief rival and boldly claimed to be king of Scotland. Few nobles supported him. Edward crushed the revolt and kidnapped Bruce's wife, the Church excommunicated him, and Bruce went into hiding on a distant North Sea island. He was now the king of nothing. Legend says he gained inspiration by watching a spider patiently build its web.

The following year, Bruce returned to Scotland and wove alliances with both nobles and the Church, slowly gaining acceptance as Scotland's king by a populace chafing under English rule. On June 24, 1314, he decisively defeated the English (now led by Edward's weak son, Edward II) at the Battle of Bannockburn. After a generation of turmoil (1286-1314), England was finally driven from Scotland, and the country was united under Robert I, king of Scotland.

As king, Robert the Bruce's priority was to stabilize the monarchy and establish clear lines of succession. His descendants would rule Scotland for the next 400 years, and even today, Bruce blood runs through the veins of Queen Elizabeth II, Prince Charles, princes William and Harry, and wee George and Charlotte.

erness of government-sponsored ad campaigns that kept the lads enlisting. Two centuries of recruiting posters make the same pitch that still works today: a hefty signing bonus, steady pay, and job security with the promise of a manly and adventurous life—all spiked with a mix of pride and patriotism.

Stepping outside the museum, you're surrounded by cannons that no longer fire, stony walls that tell an amazing story, dramatic views of this grand city, and the clatter of tourists (rather than soldiers) on cobbles. Consider for a moment all the bloody history and valiant struggles, along with British power and Scottish pride, that have shaped the city over which you are perched.

SIGHTS ON AND NEAR THE ROYAL MILE
Camera Obscura

A big deal when it was built in 1853, this observatory topped with a mirror reflected images onto a disc before the wide eyes of people

who had never seen a photograph or a captured image. Today, you can climb 100 steps for an entertaining 20-minute demonstration (3/hour). At the top, enjoy the best view anywhere of the Royal Mile. Then work your way down through five floors of illusions, holograms, and early photos. This is a big hit with kids, but very overpriced. (It's less impressive on cloudy days.)

Cost and Hours: £15, daily 9:30-19:00, July-Aug until 21:00, Sept-Oct until 20:00, tel. 0131/226-3709, www.camera-obscura. co.uk.

▲The Scotch Whisky Experience

This attraction seems designed to distill money out of your pocket. The 50-minute experience consists of a "Malt Disney" whisky-

barrel ride through the production process followed by an explanation and movie about Scotland's five main whisky regions. Though gimmicky, it does succeed in providing an entertaining yet informative orientation to the creation of Scottish firewater (things get pretty psychedelic when you hit the yeast stage). Your ticket also includes sampling a wee dram and the chance to stand amid the world's largest Scotch whisky collection (almost 3,500 bottles).

At the end, you'll find yourself in the bar, with a fascinating wall of unusually shaped whisky bottles. Serious connoisseurs should stick with the more substantial shops in town, but this place can be worthwhile for beginners. (For more on whisky and whisky tastings, see page 86).

Cost and Hours: £15 "silver tour" includes one sample, £26 "gold tour" includes samples from each main region, generally daily 10:00-18:00, tel. 0131/220-0441, www.scotchwhiskyexperience.co.uk.

▲▲Gladstone's Land

This is a typical 16th- to 17th-century merchant's "land," or tenement building. These multistory structures—in which merchants ran their shops on the ground floor and lived upstairs—were typical of the time (the word "tenement" didn't have the slum connotation then that it has today). At six stories, this one was still just half the height of the tallest "skyscrapers."

Gladstone's Land, which you'll visit via one-hour guided tour, comes complete with an almost-lived-in, furnished interior and 400-year-old Renaissance painted ceiling. The downstairs cloth shop and upstairs kitchen and living quarters are brought to life by your guide. Keep this place in mind as you stroll the rest of the Mile, imagining other houses as if they still looked like this on the inside. (For a comparison of life in the Old Town versus the New Town, also visit the Georgian House, described later.)

Cost and Hours: £7, tours run daily 10:30-16:00, 3-8 tours/day, must book ahead by phone or in person; closed Nov-March, tel. 0131/226-5856, www.nts.org.uk/Visit/Gladstones-Land.

Writers' Museum at Lady Stair's House

This aristocrat's house, built in 1622, is filled with well-described manuscripts and knickknacks of Scotland's three greatest literary figures: Robert Burns, Robert Louis Stevenson, and Sir Walter Scott. If you'd like to see Scott's pipe and Burns' snuffboxes, you'll love this little museum. You'll wind up steep staircases through a maze of rooms as you peruse first editions and keepsakes of these celebrated writers. Edinburgh's high society gathered in homes like this in the 1780s to hear the great poet Robbie Burns read his work—it's meant to be read aloud rather than to oneself (stop in the Burns room to hear his poetry).

Cost and Hours: Free, Wed-Sat 10:00-17:00, Sun from 12:00, closed Mon-Tue, tel. 0131/529-4901, www.edinburghmuseums.org.uk.

Museum on the Mound

Located in the basement of the grand Bank of Scotland building, this exhibit tells the story of the bank, which was founded in 1695 (making it only a year younger than the Bank of England, and the longest operating bank in the world). Featuring displays on cash production, safe technology, and bank robberies, this museum struggles mightily to make banking interesting (the case holding £1 million is cool). It's worth popping in if you have extra time or find the subject appealing.

Cost and Hours: Free, Tue-Fri 10:00-17:00, closed Sat-Mon, down Bank Street from the Royal Mile—follow the street around to the left and enter through the gate, tel. 0131/243-5464, www. museumonthemound.com.

▲▲St. Giles' Cathedral

This is Scotland's most important church. Its ornate spire—the Scottish crown steeple from 1495—is a proud part of Edinburgh's

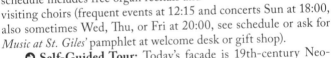

skyline. The fascinating interior contains nearly 200 memorials honoring distinguished Scots through the ages.

Cost and Hours: Free but £3 donation encouraged; Mon-Fri 9:00-19:00, Sat until 17:00; Oct-April Mon-Sat 9:00-17:00; Sun 13:00-17:00 year-round; info sheet-£1, guidebook-£6, tel. 0131/225-9442, www.stgilescathedral.org.uk.

Concerts: St. Giles' busy concert schedule includes free organ recitals and visiting choirs (frequent events at 12:15 and concerts Sun at 18:00, also sometimes Wed, Thu, or Fri at 20:00, see schedule or ask for *Music at St. Giles'* pamphlet at welcome desk or gift shop).

● Self-Guided Tour: Today's facade is 19th-century Neo-Gothic, but most of what you'll see inside is from the 14th and 15th centuries. Engage the cathedral guides in conversation; you'll be glad you did.

Just inside the entrance, turn around to see the modern stained-glass ❶ Robert Burns window, which celebrates Scotland's favorite poet (see page 60). It was made in 1985 by the Icelandic artist Leifur Breiðfjörd. The green of the lower level symbolizes the natural world—God's creation. The middle zone with the circle shows the brotherhood of man—Burns was a great internationalist. The top is a rosy red sunburst of creativity,

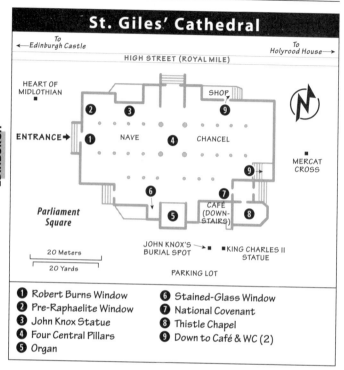

St. Giles' Cathedral

← To Edinburgh Castle

To Holyrood House →

HIGH STREET (ROYAL MILE)

HEART OF MIDLOTHIAN ■

SHOP

ENTRANCE →

NAVE

CHANCEL

■ MERCAT CROSS

Parliament Square

CAFÉ (DOWN-STAIRS)

20 Meters
20 Yards

JOHN KNOX'S BURIAL SPOT → ■

■ KING CHARLES II STATUE

PARKING LOT

❶ Robert Burns Window
❷ Pre-Raphaelite Window
❸ John Knox Statue
❹ Four Central Pillars
❺ Organ

❻ Stained-Glass Window
❼ National Covenant
❽ Thistle Chapel
❾ Down to Café & WC (2)

reminding Scots of Burns' famous line, "My love is like a red, red rose"—part of a song near and dear to every Scottish heart.

To the right of the Burns window is a fine ❷ **Pre-Raphaelite window.** Like most in the church, it's a memorial to an important patron (in this case, John Marshall). From here stretches a great swath of war memorials.

As you walk along the north wall, find ❸ **John Knox's statue** (standing like a six-foot-tall bronze chess piece). Look into his eyes for 10 seconds from 10 inches away, and think of the Reformation struggles of the 16th century. Knox, the great religious reformer and founder of austere Scottish Presbyterianism, first preached here in 1559. His insistence that every person should be able to personally read the word of God—notice that he's pointing to a book—gave Scotland an educational system 300 years ahead of the rest of Europe (for more on Knox, see

page 62). Thanks partly to Knox, it was Scottish minds that led the way in math, science, medicine, and engineering. Voltaire called Scotland "the intellectual capital of Europe."

Knox preached Calvinism. Consider that the Dutch and the Scots both embraced this creed of hard work, frugality, and strict ethics. This helps explain why the Scots are so different from the English (and why the Dutch and the Scots—both famous for their thriftiness and industriousness—are so much alike).

The oldest parts of the cathedral—the ❹ **four massive central pillars**—are Norman and date from the 12th century. They supported a mostly wooden superstructure that was lost when an invading English force burned it in 1385. The Scots rebuilt it bigger and better than ever, and in 1495 its famous crown spire was completed.

During the Reformation—when Knox preached here (1559-1572)—the place was simplified and whitewashed. Before this, when the emphasis was on holy services provided by priests, there were lots of little niches. With the new focus on sermons rather than rituals, the grand pulpit took center stage.

Knox preached against anything that separated you from God, including stained glass (considered the poor man's Bible, as illiterate Christians could learn from its pictures). Knox had the church's fancy medieval glass windows replaced with clear glass, but 19th-century Victorians took them out and installed the brilliantly colored ones you see today.

Cross over to the ❺ **organ** (1992, Austrian-built, one of Europe's finest) and take in its sheer might. (To light it up, find the button behind the organ to the right of the glass.)

Immediately to the right of the organ (as you're facing it) is a tiny chapel for silence and prayer. The dramatic ❻ **stained-glass window** above shows the commotion that surrounded Knox when

he preached. The bearded, fiery-eyed Knox had a huge impact on this community. Notice how there were no pews back then. The church was so packed, people even looked through clear windows from across the street. With his hand on the holy book, Knox seems  to conduct divine electricity to the Scottish faithful.

Find a copy of the ❼ **National Covenant** (in the corner to the far left of the organ as you face it). It was signed in blood in 1638 by Scottish heroes who refused to compromise their religion for the king's. Most who signed were martyred (their monument is nearby

Scotland's Literary Greats

Edinburgh was home to Scotland's three greatest literary figures, pictured above: Robert Burns (left), Robert Louis Stevenson (center), and Sir Walter Scott (right).

Robert Burns (1759-1796), known as "Rabbie" in Scotland and quite possibly the most famous and beloved Scot of all time, moved to Edinburgh after achieving overnight celebrity with his first volume of poetry (staying in a house on the spot where Deacon Brodie's Tavern now stands). Even though he wrote in the rough Scots dialect and dared to attack social rank, he was a favorite of Edinburgh's high society, who'd gather in fine homes to hear him recite his works.

One hundred years later, **Robert Louis Stevenson** (1850-1894) also stirred the Scottish soul with his pen. An avid traveler who always packed his notepad, Stevenson created settings that are vivid and filled with wonder. Traveling through Scotland, Europe, and around the world, he distilled his adventures into Romantic classics, including *Kidnapped* and *Treasure Island* (as well as *The Strange Case of Dr. Jekyll and Mr. Hyde*). Stevenson, who

in Grassmarket). You can see the original National Covenant in the Edinburgh Museum, described later.

Head toward the east (back) end of the church, and turn right to see the Neo-Gothic ❽ **Thistle Chapel** (£3 donation requested, volunteer guide is a wealth of information). The interior is filled with intricate wood carving. Built in two years (1910-1911), entirely with Scottish materials and labor, it is the private chapel of the Order of the Thistle, the only Scottish chivalric order. It's used several times a year for the knights to gather (and, if one dies, to inaugurate a new member). Scotland recognizes its leading citizens by bestowing a membership upon them. The Queen presides over the ritual from her fancy stall, marked by her Scottish coat of arms—a heraldic zoo of symbolism. Are there bagpipes in heaven?

was married in San Francisco and spent his last years in the South Pacific, wrote, "Youth is the time to travel—both in mind and in body—to try the manners of different nations." He said, "I travel not to go anywhere...but to simply go." Travel was his inspiration and his success.

Sir Walter Scott (1771-1832) wrote the *Waverley* novels, including *Ivanhoe* and *Rob Roy*. He's considered the father of the Romantic historical novel. Through his writing, he generated a worldwide interest in Scotland, and reawakened his fellow countrymen's pride in their heritage. His novels helped revive interest in Highland culture—the Gaelic language, kilts, songs, legends, myths, the clan system—and created a national identity. An avid patriot, he wrote, "Every Scottish man has a pedigree. It is a national prerogative, as unalienable as his pride and his poverty." Scott is so revered in Edinburgh that his towering Neo-Gothic monument dominates the city center. With his favorite hound by his side, Sir Walter Scott overlooks the city that he inspired, and that inspired him.

The best way to learn about and experience these literary greats is to visit the Writers' Museum at Lady Stair's House (see page 56) and to take Edinburgh's Literary Pub Tour (see page 94).

While just three writers dominate your Edinburgh sightseeing, consider also the other great writers with Edinburgh connections: J. K. Rowling (who captures the "Gothic" spirit of Edinburgh with her Harry Potter series); current resident Ian Rankin (with his "tartan noir" novels); J. M. Barrie (who attended University of Edinburgh and later created Peter Pan); Sir Arthur Conan Doyle (who was born in Edinburgh, went to medical school here, and is best known for inventing Sherlock Holmes); and James Boswell (who lived 50 yards away from the Writers' Museum, in James Court, and is revered for his biography of Samuel Johnson).

Find the tooting stone angel at the top of a window to the left of the altar, and the wooden one to the right of the doorway you came in.

❾ **Downstairs** you'll find handy public WCs and an inviting **$ café**—a good place for paupers to munch prayerfully (simple, light lunches, coffee and cakes; Mon-Sat 9:00-17:00, Sun from 11:00, in basement on back side of church, tel. 0131/225-5147).

Old Parliament House

The building now holds the civil law courts, so you'll need to go through security first. Peruse the info panels in the grand hall, with its fine 1639 hammer-beam ceiling and stained glass. This space housed the Scottish parliament until the Act of Union in 1707. The biggest stained-glass window depicts the initiation of the first Scottish High Court in 1532. The building now holds the civil law courts and is busy with wigged and robed lawyers hard at work in the old library (peek through the door) or pacing the hall deep in discussion. The basement café is literally their supreme court's restaurant (open to public until 14:30).

Cost and Hours: Free, public welcome Mon-Fri 9:00-16:30, closed Sat-Sun, no photos, enter behind St. Giles' Cathedral at door #11; open-to-the-public trials are just across the street at the High Court—the doorman has the day's docket.

▲The Real Mary King's Close

For an unusual peek at Edinburgh's gritty, plague-ridden past, join a costumed performer on an hour-long trip through an excavated underground street and buildings on the northern slope of the Royal Mile. Tours cover the standard goofy, crowd-pleasing ghost stories, but also provide authentic and historical insight into a part of town entombed by later construction. It's best to book ahead (online up to the day before, or by phone or in person for a same-day booking)—even though tours leave every 15-30 minutes, groups are small and the sight is popular.

Cost and Hours: £15; daily 10:00-21:00, Nov-March Sun-Thu until 17:00; these are last tour times, across from St. Giles' at 2 Warriston's Close—but enter through well-marked door facing High Street, tel. 0845-070-6244, www.realmarykingsclose.com.

▲Museum of Childhood

This five-story playground of historical toys and games is rich in nostalgia and history. Each well-signed gallery is as jovial as a Norman Rockwell painting, highlighting the delights and simplicity of childhood. The museum does a fair job of representing culturally relevant oddities, such as ancient Egyptian, Peruvian, and voodoo dolls, and displays early versions of toys it's probably best didn't make the final cut (such as a grim snake-centered precursor to the popular board game Chutes and Ladders).

Cost and Hours: Free, Thu-Mon 10:00-17:00 except Sun from 12:00, closed Tue-Wed, 42 High Street.

John Knox House

Intriguing for Reformation buffs, this fine medieval house dates back to 1470 and offers a well-explained look at the life of the great 16th-century reformer. Although most contend he never actually lived here, preservationists called it "Knox's house" to save it from the wrecking ball in the 1840s. Regardless, the place has good information on Knox and his intellectual sparring

partner, Mary, Queen of Scots. Imagine the Protestant firebrand John Knox and the devout Catholic Mary sitting face-to-face in old rooms like these, discussing the most intimate matters of their spiritual lives as they decided the course of Scotland's religious future. The sparsely furnished house contains some period furniture, an early 1600s hand-painted ceiling, information on the house and its resident John Mossman (goldsmith to Mary, Queen of Scots), and exhibits on printing—an essential tool for early reformers.

Cost and Hours: £5, Mon-Sat 10:00-18:00, closed Sun except in July-Aug 12:00-18:00, 43 High Street, tel. 0131/556-9579, www.tracscotland.org.

▲People's Story Museum

This engaging exhibit traces the working and social lives of ordinary people through the 18th, 19th, and 20th centuries. You'll see tools, products, and objects related to important Edinburgh trades (printing, brewing), a wartime kitchen, and a circa-1989 trip to the movies. On the top floor, a dated but endearing 22-minute film offers insight into the ways people have lived in this city for generations. On the ground floor, peek into the former jail, an original part of the historic building (the Canongate Tolbooth, built in 1591).

Cost and Hours: Free, Wed-Sat 10:00-17:00 except Sun from 12:00, closed Mon-Tue, 163 Canongate, tel. 0131/529-4057, www.edinburghmuseums.org.uk.

▲Museum of Edinburgh

Another old house full of old stuff, this one is worth a stop for a look at its early Edinburgh history (and its handy ground-floor WC). Be sure to see the original copy of the National Covenant—written in 1638 on animal skin. Scottish leaders signed this, refusing to adopt the king's religion—and were killed because of it. Exploring the rest of the collection, keep an eye out for Robert Louis Stevenson's antique golf ball, James Craig's architectural plans for the Georgian New Town, an interactive kids' area with dress-up clothes, a sprawling top-floor exhibit on Edinburgh-born Field Marshall Sir David Haig (who led the British Western Front efforts in World War I and later became Earl Haig), and locally made glass and ceramics.

Cost and Hours: Free, Thu-Mon 10:00-17:00 except Sun from 12:00, closed Tue-Wed, 142 Canongate, tel. 0131/529-4143, www.edinburghmuseums.org.uk.

EDINBURGH

▲▲Scottish Parliament Building

Scotland's parliament originated in 1293 and was dissolved when Scotland united with England in 1707. But after the Scottish electorate and the British parliament gave their consent, in 1997 it was decided that there should again be "a Scottish parliament guided by justice, wisdom, integrity, and compassion." Formally reconvened by Queen Elizabeth II in 1999, the Scottish parliament now enjoys self-rule in many areas (except for matters of defense, foreign policy, immigration, and taxation). The current

government, run by the Scottish Nationalist Party (SNP), is pushing for even more independence.

The innovative building, opened in 2004, brought together all the functions of the fledgling parliament in one complex. It's a people-oriented structure (conceived by Catalan architect Enric Miralles). Signs are written in both English and Gaelic (the Scots' Celtic tongue).

For a peek at the building and a lesson in how the Scottish parliament works, drop in, pass through security, and find the visi-

tors' desk. You're welcome in the public parts of the building, including a small ground-floor exhibit on the parliament's history and function and, up several flights of stairs, a viewing gallery overlooking the impressive Debating Chambers.

Cost and Hours: Free; Mon-Sat 10:00-17:00, Tue-Thu 9:00-18:30 when parliament is in session (Sept-June), closed Sun year-round. For a complete list of recess dates or to book tickets for debates, check their website or call their visitor services line, tel. 0131/348-5200, www.parliament. scot.

Tours: Free worthwhile hour-long tours covering history, architecture, parliamentary processes, and other topics are offered by proud locals. Tours generally run throughout the day Mon and Fri-Sat in session (Sept-June) and Mon-Sat in recess (July-Aug). While you can try dropping in, these tours can book up—it's best to book ahead online or over the phone.

Seeing Parliament in Session: The public can witness the Scottish parliament's hugely popular debates (usually Tue-Thu 14:00-18:00; book ahead online, over the phone, or at the info desk).

On Thursdays from 11:40 to 12:45 the First Minister is on the hot seat and has to field questions from members across all parties (reserve ahead for this popular session over the phone a week in advance; spots book up quickly—call at 9:00 sharp on Thu for the following week).

▲▲Palace of Holyroodhouse

Built on the site of the abbey/monastery founded in 1128 by King David I, this palace was the true home, birthplace, and corona-

tion spot of Scotland's Stuart kings in their heyday (James IV; Mary, Queen of Scots; and Charles I). It's particularly memorable as the site of some dramatic moments from the short reign of Mary, Queen of Scots—including the murder of her personal secretary, David Rizzio, by agents of her jealous husband. Today, it's one of Queen Elizabeth II's official residences. She usually manages her Scottish affairs here during Holyrood Week, from late June to early July (and generally stays at Balmoral in August). Holyrood is open to the public outside of the Queen's visits. Touring the interior offers a more polished contrast to Edinburgh Castle, and is particularly worth considering if you don't plan to go to Balmoral. The one-way audioguide route leads you through the fine apartments and tells some of the notable stories that played out here.

Cost: £12.50, includes quality one-hour audioguide; £17.50 combo-ticket includes the Queen's Gallery; £21.50 combo-ticket adds guided tour of palace gardens (April-Oct only); tickets sold in Queen's Gallery to the right of the castle entrance (see next listing).

Hours: Daily 9:30-18:00, Nov-March until 16:30, last entry 1.5 hours before closing, tel. 0131/556-5100, www.royalcollection.org.uk. It's still a working palace, so it's closed when the Queen or other VIPs are in residence.

Visiting the Palace: The building, rich in history and decor, is filled with elegantly furnished Victorian rooms and a few darker, older rooms with glass cases of historic bits and Scottish pieces that locals find fascinating. Bring the palace to life with the audioguide. The tour route leads you into the grassy inner courtyard, then up to the royal apartments: dining rooms, *Downton Abbey*-style drawing rooms, and royal bedchambers. Along the way, you'll learn the story behind the 96 portraits of Scottish leaders (some real, others imaginary) that line the Great Gallery; why the king never slept in his official "state bed"; why the exiled Comte d'Artois took refuge in the palace; and how the current Queen puts her Scottish subjects at ease when she receives them here. Finally, you'll twist up a tight spiral staircase to the private chambers of Mary, Queen of Scots, where conspirators stormed in and stabbed her secretary 56 times.

After exiting the palace, you're free to stroll through the evocative **ruined abbey** (destroyed by the English during the time of Mary, Queen of Scots, in the 16th century) and the **palace gardens** (closed Nov-March except some weekends). Some 8,000 guests—including many honored ladies sporting fancy hats—gather here every July when the Queen hosts a magnificent tea party. (She gets help pouring.)

Nearby: Hikers, note that the wonderful trail up Arthur's Seat starts just across the street from the gardens (see page 83 for details).

Queen's Gallery

This small museum features rotating exhibits of artwork from the royal collection. For more than five centuries, the royal family has

amassed a wealth of art treasures. While the Queen keeps most in her many private palaces, she shares an impressive load of it here, with exhibits changing about every six months. Though the gallery occupies just a few rooms, its displays can be exquisite. The entry fee includes an excellent audioguide, written and read by the curator.

Cost and Hours: £7, £17.50 combo-ticket includes Palace of Holyroodhouse, daily 9:30-18:00, Nov-March until 16:30, last entry one hour before closing, café, on the palace grounds, to the right of the palace entrance, www.royalcollection.org.uk. Buses #35 and #36 stop outside, saving you a walk to or from Princes Street/North Bridge.

Our Dynamic Earth

Located about a five-minute walk from the Palace of Holyroodhouse, this immense exhibit tells the story of our planet, filling several underground floors under a vast, white Gore-Tex tent. It's pitched, appropriately, at the base of the Salisbury Crags. The exhibit is designed for younger

kids and does the same thing an American science exhibit would do—but with a charming Scottish accent. You'll learn about the Scottish geologists who pioneered the discipline, then step into a "time machine" to watch the years rewind, from cave dwellers to dinosaurs to the Big Bang. After viewing several short films on stars, tectonic plates, ice caps, and worldwide weather (in a "4-D" exhibit), you're free to wander past salty pools and a re-created rain forest.

Cost and Hours: £15, kids-£9.50, daily 10:00-17:30, July-Aug until 18:00, closed Mon-Tue Nov-March, last entry 1.5 hours before closing, on Holyrood Road, between the palace and mountain, tel. 0131/550-7800, www.dynamicearth.co.uk.

SIGHTS SOUTH OF THE ROYAL MILE

▲▲▲National Museum of Scotland

This huge museum has amassed more historic artifacts than every other place I've seen in Scotland combined. It's all wonderfully displayed, with fine descriptions offering a best-anywhere hike through the history of Scotland.

Cost and Hours: Free, daily 10:00-17:00; two long blocks south of St. Giles' Cathedral and the Royal Mile, on Chambers Street off George IV Bridge, tel. 0131/247-4422, www.nms.ac.uk.

Tours: Free one-hour general tours are offered daily at 11:00 and 13:00; themed tours at 15:00 (confirm tour schedule at info desk or on TV screens). The National Museum of Scotland Highlights app provides thin coverage of select items but is free and downloadable using their free Wi-Fi.

Eating: A **$$ brasserie** is on the ground floor near the information desks, and a **$ café** with coffee, tea, cakes, and snacks is on the level 3 balcony overlooking the Grand Gallery. On the museum's fifth floor, the dressy and upscale **$$$ Tower restaurant** serves good food with a castle view (lunch/early-bird special, afternoon tea, three-course dinner specials; daily 10:00-22:00—use Tower entry if eating after museum closes, reservations recommended, tel. 0131/225-3003, www.tower-restaurant.com). A number of good eating options are within a couple of blocks of the museum (see page 107).

Overview: The place gives you two museums in one. One wing houses the Natural World galleries (T. Rex skeletons and other animals), the Science and Technology galleries, and a fashion exhibit. (The museum's Ancient Egypt and East Asia collections are currently under renovation.) With time and interest, these are all worth a look. But we'll focus on the other wing, which sweeps you through Scottish history covering Roman and Viking times, Edinburgh's witch-burning craze and clan massacres, the struggle for Scottish independence, the Industrial Revolution, and right up to Scotland in the 21st century.

○ Self-Guided Tour: Get oriented on level 1, in the impressive glass-roofed Grand Gallery right above the entrance hall. Just outside the Grand Gallery is the **millennium clock,** a 30-foot high clock with figures that move to a Bach concerto on the hour from 11:00 to 16:00. The clock has four parts (crypt, nave, belfry, and spire) and represents the turmoil of the 20th century, with a pietà at the top.

• *To reach the Scottish history wing, exit the Grand Gallery at the far right end, under the clock and past the statue of James Watt.*

On the way, you'll pass through the science and technology wing. While walking through, look for **Dolly the sheep**—the world's first cloned mammal—born in Edinburgh and now stuffed and on display. Continue into Hawthornden Court (level 1), where our tour begins. (It's possible to detour downstairs from here to level -1 for Scotland's prehistoric origins—geologic formation, Celts, Romans, Vikings.)

• *Enter the door marked...*

Kingdom of the Scots (c. 1300-1700): From its very start, Scotland was determined to be free. You're greeted with proud quotes from what's been called the Scottish Declaration of Independence—the Declaration of Arbroath, a defiant letter written to the pope in 1320. As early as the ninth century, Scotland's patron saint, Andrew (see the small statue in the next room), had—according to legend—miraculously intervened to help the Picts and Scots of Scotland remain free by defeating the Angles of England. Andrew's X-shaped cross still decorates the Scottish flag today.

Enter the first room on your right, with imposing swords and other objects related to Scotland's most famous patriots—William Wallace and Robert the Bruce. Bruce's descendants, the Stuarts, went on to rule Scotland for the next 300 years. Eventually, James VI of Scotland (see his baby cradle) came to rule England as well (as King James I of England).

In the next room, a big guillotine recalls the harsh justice meted out to criminals, witches, and "Covenanters" (17th-century political activists who opposed interference of the Stuart kings in affairs of the Presbyterian Church of Scotland). Nearby, also check out the tomb (a copy) of Mary,

Queen of Scots, the 16th-century Stuart monarch who opposed the Presbyterian Church of Scotland. Educated and raised in Renaissance France, Mary brought refinement to the Scottish throne. After she was imprisoned and then executed by Elizabeth I of England in 1587, her supporters rallied each other by invoking her memory. Pendants and coins with her portrait stoked the irrepressible Scottish spirit (see display case near tomb).

Browse the rest of level 1 to see everyday objects from that age: carved panels, cookware, and clothes.

• *Backtrack to Hawthornden Court and head up to level 3.*

Scotland Transformed (1700s): You'll see artifacts related to Bonnie Prince Charlie and the Jacobite rebellions as well as the ornate Treaty of Union document, signed in 1707 by the Scottish parliament. This act voluntarily united Scotland with England under the single parliament of the United Kingdom. For some Scots, this move was an inevitable step in connecting to the wider world, but for others it symbolized the end of Scotland's existence.

Union with England brought stability and investment to Scotland. In this same era, the advances of the Industrial Revolution were making a big impact on Scottish life. Mechanized textile looms (on display) replaced hand craftsmanship. The huge Newcomen steam-engine water pump helped the mining industry to develop sites with tricky drainage. Nearby is a model of a coal mine (or "colliery"); coal-rich Scotland exploited this natural resource to fuel its textile factories.

How the parsimonious Scots financed these new, large-scale enterprises is explained in an exhibit on the Bank of Scotland. Powered by the Scottish work ethic and the new opportunities that came from the Industrial Revolution, the country came into relative prosperity. Education and medicine thrived. With the dawn of the modern age came leisure time, the concept of "healthful sports," and golf—a popular Scottish pastime. On display (near the back, behind the machinery) are some early golf balls, which date from about 1820, made of leather and stuffed with feathers.

• *Journey up to level 5.*

Industry and Empire (1800s): Turn right and do a counterclockwise spin around this floor to survey Scottish life in the 19th century. Industry had transformed the country. Highland farmers left their land to find work in Lowland factories and foundries. Modern inventions—the phonograph, the steam-powered train, the kitchen range—revolutionized everyday life. In Glasgow near the turn of the century, architect Charles Rennie Mackintosh helped to define Scottish Art Nouveau. Scotland was at the forefront of literature (Robert Burns, Sir Walter Scott, Robert Louis Stevenson), science (Lord Kelvin, James Watt, Alexander Graham Bell...he was born here, anyway!), world exploration (John Kirk in Africa, Sir Alexander Mackenzie in Canada), and whisky production.

• *Climb the stairs to level 6.*

Scotland: A Changing Nation (1900s): Turn left and do a clockwise spin through this floor to bring the story to the present day. The two world wars decimated the population of this already wee nation. In addition, hundreds of thousands emigrated, especially to Canada (where one in eight Canadians has Scottish origins). Other exhibits include Scots in the world of entertainment (from early boy-band Bay City Rollers to actor-comedian Billy Connolly); a look at the recent trend of devolution from the United Kingdom (1999 opening of Scotland's own parliament and the landmark 2014 referendum on Scottish independence); and a sports Hall of Fame (from golfer Tom Morris to auto racers Jackie Stewart and Jim Clark).

• *Finish your visit on level 7, the rooftop.*

Garden Terrace: The well-described roof garden features grasses and heathers from every corner of Scotland and spectacular views of the city.

Greyfriars Bobby Statue and Greyfriars Cemetery

This famous **statue** of Edinburgh's favorite dog is across the street from the National Museum of Scotland. Every business nearby, it seems, is named for this Victorian Skye terrier, who is reputed to have stood by his master's grave in Greyfriars Cemetery for 14 years. The story was immortalized in a 1960s Disney flick, but recent research suggests that 19th-century business-

men bribed a stray to hang out in the cemetery to attract sightseers. If it was a ruse, it still works.

Just behind Bobby is the entrance to his namesake **cemetery**. Stepping through the gate, you'll see the pink-marble grave of Bobby himself. The well-tended cemetery is an evocative place to stroll, and a nice escape from the city's bustle. Harry Potter fans could turn it into a scavenger hunt: J. K. Rowling sketched out her saga just around the corner at The Elephant House café—and a few of the cemetery's weather-beaten headstones bear familiar names, including McGonagall and Thomas Riddell. Beyond the cemetery fence are the frilly Gothic spires of posh George Heriot's School, said to have inspired Hogwarts. And just a few short blocks to the east is a street called...Potterrow.

EDINBURGH

Grassmarket

Once Edinburgh's site for hangings (residents rented out their windows—above the rudely named "Last Drop" pub—for the

view), today Grassmarket is a people-friendly piazza. It was originally the city's garage, a depot for horses and cows (hence the name). It's rowdy here at night—a popular place for "hen dos" and "stag dos" (bachelorette and bachelor parties). In the early evening, the Literary Pub Tour departs from here (see page 94). Some good shopping

streets branch off from Grassmarket: Victoria Street, built in the Victorian Age, is lined with colorful little shops and eateries; angling off in the other direction, Candlemaker's Row has a few interesting artisan shops (and leads, in just a couple minutes' walk, up to Greyfriars Bobby and the National Museum; for more shopping tips in this area, see page 88).

At the top of Grassmarket is the round monument to the "Covenanters." These strict 17th-century Scottish Protestants were killed for refusing to accept the king's Episcopalian prayer book. To this day, Scots celebrate their national church's emphatically democratic government. Rather than big-shot bishops (as in the Anglican or Roman Catholic Church), they have a low-key "moderator" who's elected each year.

MUSEUMS IN THE NEW TOWN

These sights are linked by the "Bonnie Wee New Town Walk" on page 38.

▲▲Scottish National Gallery

This delightful, small museum has Scotland's best collection of paintings. In a short visit,

you can admire well-described works by Old Masters (Raphael, Rembrandt, Rubens), Impressionists (Monet, Degas, Gauguin), and a few underrated Scottish painters. (Scottish art is better at the National Portrait Gallery, described next.) Although there are no iconic masterpieces, it's a surprisingly enjoyable collection that's truly world-class.

Cost and Hours: Free; daily 10:00-17:00, Thu until 19:00, longer hours in Aug; café downstairs, The Mound (between Princes and Market streets), tel. 0131/624-6200, www.nationalgalleries.org.

Expect Changes: The museum is undergoing major renovation to increase the space of its Scottish collection and build a grand main entrance from Princes Street Gardens. As a result, certain exhibits may be closed, and pieces may be relocated, on loan, or in storage. Ask one of the friendly tartan-sporting attendants or at the info desk downstairs (near the WCs and gallery shop) if you can't find a particular item.

Next Door: The skippable **Royal Scottish Academy** hosts temporary art exhibits and is connected to the Scottish National Gallery at the Gardens level (underneath the gallery) by the Weston Link building (same hours as gallery, fine café and restaurant).

Visiting the Museum: Start at the gallery entrance (at the north end of the building). Climb the stairs to the upper level (north end), and take a left. You'll run right into...

Van der Goes, *The Trinity Panels,* c. 1473-1479: For more

than five centuries, these two double-sided panels have remained here—first in a church, then (when the church was leveled to build Waverley train station) in this museum. The panels likely were the wings of a triptych, flanking a central scene of the Virgin Mary that was destroyed by Protestant vandals during the Reformation.

In one panel is the Trinity: God the Father, in a rich red robe, cradles a spindly, just-crucified Christ, while the dove of the Holy Spirit hovers between them. (This is what would have been seen when the triptych was closed.) The flip side of the Christ panel depicts Scotland's king and queen, who are best known to history as the parents of the boy kneeling alongside them. He grew up to become James IV, the Renaissance king who made Edinburgh a cultural capital. On the other panel, the church's director (the man who commissioned the painting from the well-known Flemish painter) kneels and looks on while an angel plays a hymn on the church organ. On the opposite side is Margaret of Denmark, Queen of Scots, being presented by a saint.

In typically medieval fashion, the details are meticulous—expressive faces, intricate folds in the robes, Christ's pallid skin, observant angels. The donor's face is a remarkable portrait, with realistic skin tone and a five-o'clock shadow. But the painting lacks true 3-D realism—God's gold throne is overly exaggerated, and Christ's cardboard-cutout body hovers weightlessly.

• *Go back across the top of the skylight, to a room where the next two paintings hang.*

Botticelli, *The Virgin Adoring the Sleeping Christ Child,* c. 1485: Mary looks down at her baby, peacefully sleeping in a flower-filled garden. It's easy to appreciate Botticelli's masterful style: the precisely drawn outlines, the Virgin's pristine skin, the translucent glow. Botticelli creates a serene world in which no shadows are cast. The scene is painted on canvas—unusual at a time when wood panels were the norm. For the Virgin's rich cloak, Botticelli used ground-up lapis lazuli (a very pricey semiprecious stone), and her hem is decorated with gold leaf.

Renaissance-era art lovers would instantly catch the symbolism. Mary wears a wispy halo and blue cloak that recalls the sky blue of heaven. The roses without thorns and enclosed garden are both symbols of virginity, while the violet flowers (at bottom) represent humility. Darker symbolism hints at what's to come. The strawberries (lower right) signify Christ's blood, soon to be shed, while the roses—though thornless now—will become the Crown of Thorns. For now, Mary can adore her sleeping, blissful baby in a peaceful garden. But in a few decades she'll be kneeling again to weep over the dead, crucified Messiah.

Raphael, *Holy Family with a Palm Tree,* 1506-1507: Mary, Joseph, and the Christ Child fit snugly within a round frame (a tondo), their pose symbolizing geometric perfection and the perfect family unit. Joseph kneels to offer Jesus flowers. Mary curves toward him. Baby Jesus dangles in between, linking the family together. Raphael also connects the

figures through eye contact: Mary eyes Joseph, who locks onto Jesus, who gazes precociously back. Like in a cameo, we see the faces incised in profile, while their bodies bulge out toward us.

• *Back downstairs at ground level is the main gallery space. Circle around the collection chronologically, watching for works by Bellini, Titian, Velázquez, and El Greco. In Room 7, look for the next two paintings.*

Rubens, *Feast of Herod*, c. 1635-1638: All eyes turn to watch the dramatic culmination of the story of John the Baptist. Salome (standing in center) presents John's severed head on a platter to a horrified King Herod, who clutches the tablecloth and buries his hand in his beard to stifle a gag. Meanwhile, Herod's wife—who cooked up the nasty plot—pokes spitefully at John's head with a fork. A dog tugs at Herod's foot like a nasty conscience. The canvas—big, colorful, full of motion and drama—is totally Baroque. Some have suggested that the features of Herod's wife and Salome are those of Rubens' wife and ex-wives, and the head is Rubens himself.

Rembrandt, *Self-Portrait, Aged 51*, c. 1657: It's 1657, and 51-year-old Rembrandt has just declared bankruptcy. Besides financial hardship and the auctioning-off of his personal belongings, he's also facing social stigma and behind-his-back ridicule. Once Holland's most renowned painter, he's begun a slow decline into poverty and obscurity.

His face says it all. Holding a steady gaze, he stares with matter-of-fact acceptance, with his lips pursed. He's dressed in dark clothes against a dark background, with the only spot of light shining on the worry lines of his forehead. Get close enough to the canvas to see the thick paste of paint he used for the wrinkles around his eyes—a study in aging.

• *In Room 11, find...*

Gainsborough, *The Honorable Mrs. Graham*, 1775-1777: The slender, elegant, lavishly dressed woman was the teenage bride of a wealthy Scottish landowner. She leans on a column, ostrich feather in hand, staring off to the side (Thoughtfully? Determinedly? Haughtily?). Her faultless face and smooth neck stand out from the elaborately ruffled dress and background foliage. This 18th-century woman wears a silvery dress that echoes 17th-century style—Gainsborough's way of showing how, though she was young, she was classy. Thomas ("Blue Boy") Gainsborough—the product of a clothes-making father and a flower-painting mother—uses aspects of both in this lush portrait.

The ruby brooch on her bodice marks the center of this harmonious composition.

• *Climb the stairs to the upper level (south end, opposite from where you entered) and turn right for the Impressionists and Post-Impressionists.*

Impressionist Collection: The gallery has a smattering of (mostly smaller-scale) works from all the main artists of the Impressionist and Post-Impressionist eras. You'll see Degas' ballet scenes, Renoir's pastel-colored family scenes, Van Gogh's peasants, and Seurat's pointillism.

• *Keep an eye out for these three paintings.*

Monet's *Poplars on the River Epte* (1891) was part of the artist's famous "series" paintings. He set up several canvases in a floating studio near his home in Giverny. He'd start on one canvas in the morning (to catch the morning light), then move to the next as the light changed. This particular canvas captures a perfect summer day, showing both the poplars on the riverbank and their mirror image in the still water. The subject matter begins to dissolve into a pure pattern of color, anticipating abstract art.

Gauguin's *Vision of the Sermon* (1888) shows French peasant women imagining the miraculous event they've just heard preached about in church—when Jacob wrestles with an angel. The painting is a watershed in art history, as Gauguin throws out the rules of "realism" that had reigned since the Renaissance. The colors are surreal, there are no shadows, the figures are arranged almost randomly, and there's no attempt to make the wrestlers appear distant. The diagonal tree branch is the only thing separating the everyday world from the miraculous. Later, when Gauguin moved to Tahiti (see his *Three Tahitians* nearby), he painted a similar world, where the everyday and magical coexist, with symbolic power.

Sargent's *Lady Agnew of Lochnaw* (1892) is the work that launched the career of this American-born portrait artist. Lady Agnew—the young wife of a wealthy old Scotsman—lounges back languidly and gazes out self-assuredly. The Impressionistic smudges of paint on her dress and the chair contrast with her clear skin and luminous eyeballs. Her relaxed pose (one arm hanging down the side) contrasts with her intensity: head tilted slightly down while she gazes up, a corner of her mouth askew, and an eyebrow cocked seductively.

Scottish Collection: The museum is undergoing a major renovation to build a larger and better

EDINBURGH

home for this collection. Until then, look for the following artists scattered around the main gallery.

Allan Ramsay, the son of the well-known poet of the same name, painted portraits of curly-wigged men of the Enlightenment era (the philosopher David Hume, King George III) as well as likenesses of his two wives. Ramsay's portrait of the duke of Argyll—founder of the Royal Bank of Scotland—appears on the front of notes printed by this bank.

Sir Henry Raeburn chronicled the next generation: Sir Walter Scott, the proud kilt-wearing Alastair MacDonell, and the ice-skating Reverend Robert Walker, minister of the Canongate Church.

Sir David Wilkie's forte was small-scale scenes of everyday life. *The Letter of Introduction* (1813) captures Wilkie's own experience of trying to impress skeptical art patrons in London; even the dog is sniffing the Scotsman out. *Distraining for Rent* (1815) shows the plight of a poor farmer about to lose his farm—a common occurrence during 19th-century industrialization.

William Dyce's *Francesca da Rimini* (1837) depicts star-crossed lovers—a young wife and her husband's kid brother—who can't help but indulge their passion. The husband later finds out and kills her; at the far left, you see his ominous hand.

William McTaggart's impressionistic landscape scenes from the late 1800s provide a glimpse of the unique light, powerful clouds, and natural wonder of the Highlands.

▲▲Scottish National Portrait Gallery

Put a face on Scotland's history by enjoying these portraits of famous Scots from the earliest times until today. From its Neo-Gothic facade to a grand entry hall featuring a *Who's Who* of Scotland, to galleries highlighting the great Scots of each age, this impressive museum will fascinate anyone interested in Scottish culture. The gallery also hosts temporary exhibits highlighting the work of more contemporary Scots. Because of its purely Scottish focus, many travelers prefer this to the (pan-European) main branch of the National Gallery.

Cost and Hours: Free, daily 10:00-17:00, good **$** cafeteria serving healthy meals, 1 Queen Street, tel. 0131/624-6490, www.nationalgalleries.org.

Visiting the Gallery: In the stirring **entrance hall** you'll find busts of great Scots and a full-body statue of Robbie "Rabbie" Burns, as well as (up above) a glorious frieze showing a parade of historical figures and murals depicting important events in Scottish history. (These are better viewed from the first floor and its mezzanine—described later.) We'll start on the **second floor,** right into the thick of the struggle between Scotland and England over who should rule this land.

Reformation to Revolution (gallery 1): The collection starts with a portrait of **Mary, Queen of Scots** (1542-1587), her cross and rosary prominent. This controversial ruler set off two centuries of strife. Mary was born with both Stuart blood (the ruling family of Scotland) and the Tudor blood of England's monarchs (Queen Elizabeth I was her cousin). Catholic and French-educated, Mary felt alienated from her own increasingly Protestant homeland. Her tense conversations with the reformer John Knox must have been epic. Then came a series of scandals: She married unpopular Lord Darnley, then (possibly) cheated on him, causing Darnley to (possibly) murder her lover, causing

Mary to (possibly) murder Darnley, then (possibly) run off with another man, and (possibly) plot against Queen Elizabeth.

Amid all that drama, Mary was forced by her own people to relinquish her throne to her infant son, **James VI.** Find his portraits as a child and as a grown-up. James grew up to rule Scotland, and when Queen Elizabeth (the "virgin queen") died without an heir, he also became king of England (James I). But James' son, **Charles I,** after a bitter civil war, was arrested and executed in 1649: See the large *Execution of Charles I* painting high on the far wall, his blood-dripping head displayed to the crowd; nearby is a portrait of Charles in happier times, as a 12-year-old boy. His son, Charles II, restored the Stuarts to power. He was then succeeded by his Catholic brother James VII of Scotland (II of England), who was sent into exile in France. There the Stuarts stewed, planning a return to power, waiting for someone to lead them in what would come to be known as the Jacobite rebellions.

The Jacobite Cause (gallery 4): One of the biggest paintings in the room is *The Baptism of Prince Charles Edward Stuart.* Born in 1720, this Stuart heir to the thrones of Great Britain and Ireland is better known to history as "Bonnie Prince Charlie." (See his bonnie features in various portraits nearby, as a child, young

man, and grown man.) Charismatic Charles convinced France to invade Scotland and put him back on the throne there. In 1745, he entered Edinburgh in triumph. But he was defeated at the tide-turning Battle of Culloden (1746). The Stuart cause died forever, and Bonnie Prince Charlie went into exile, eventually dying drunk and wasted in Rome, far from the land he nearly ruled.

• *The next few rooms (galleries 5-6) contain special exhibits that swap out every year or two—they're worth a browse.*

The Age of Improvement (gallery 7): The faces portrayed here belonged to a new society whose hard work and public spirit achieved progress with a Scottish accent. Social equality and the Industrial Revolution "transformed" Scotland—you'll see portraits of the great poet Robert Burns, the son of a farmer (Burns was heralded as a "heaven-taught ploughman" when his poems were first published), and the man who perfected the steam engine, James Watt.

• *Check out the remaining galleries, with more special exhibits, then head back down to the first floor for a good look at the...*

Central Atrium (first floor): Great Scots! The atrium is decorated in a parade of late-19th-century Romantic Historicism. The **frieze** (working counterclockwise) is a visual encyclopedia, from an ax-wielding Stone Age man and a druid, to the early legendary monarchs (Macbeth), to warriors William Wallace and Robert the Bruce, to many kings (James I, II, III, and so on), to great think-ers, inventors, and artists (Allan Ramsay, Flora MacDonald, David Hume, Adam Smith, James Boswell, James Watt), the three greatest Scot-tish writers (Robert Burns, Sir Wal-ter Scott, Robert Louis Stevenson), and culminating with the historian Thomas Carlyle, who was the driv-ing spirit (powered by the fortune of a local newspaper baron) behind creating this portrait gallery.

Around the first-floor mezzanine are large-scale **murals** de-picting great events in Scottish history, including the landing of St. Margaret at Queensferry in 1068, the Battle of Stirling Bridge in 1297, the Battle of Bannockburn in 1314, and the marriage procession of James IV and Margaret Tudor through the streets of Edinburgh in 1503.

• *Also on this floor you'll find the...*

Modern Portrait Gallery: This space is dedicated to rotating art and photographs highlighting Scots who are making an impact in the world today, such as Annie Lennox, Alan Cumming, and physicist Peter Higgs (theorizer of the Higgs boson, the so-called God particle). Look for the *Three Oncologists*, a ghostly painting depicting the anxiety and terror of cancer and the dedication of those working so hard to conquer it.

▲▲Georgian House

This refurbished Neoclassical house, set on Charlotte Square, is a trip back to 1796. It recounts the era when a newly gentrified and well-educated Edinburgh was nicknamed the "Athens of the North." Begin on the second floor, where you'll watch an interesting 16-minute video dramatizing the upstairs/downstairs lifestyles of the aristocrats and servants who lived here. Try on some Georgian outfits, then head downstairs to tour period rooms and even peek into the fully stocked medicine cabinet. Info sheets are available in each room, along with volunteer guides who share stories and trivia, such as why Georgian bigwigs had to sit behind a screen while enjoying a fire. A walk down George Street after your visit here can be fun for the imagination.

Cost and Hours: £7.50, daily 10:00-17:00, March and Nov 11:00-16:00, closed Dec-Feb, last entry 45 minutes before closing; 7 Charlotte Square, tel. 0131/226-3318, www.nts.org.uk.

SIGHTS NEAR EDINBURGH

▲▲Royal Yacht *Britannia*

This much-revered vessel, which transported Britain's royal family for more than 40 years on 900 voyages (an average of once around the world per year) before being retired in 1997, is permanently moored in Edinburgh's port of Leith. Queen Elizabeth II said of the ship, "This is the only place I can truly relax." Today it's open to the curious public, who have access to its many decks—from engine rooms to drawing rooms—and offers a fascinating time-warp look into the late-20th-century lifestyles of the rich and royal. It's worth the 20-minute bus or taxi ride from the center; figure on spending about 2.5 hours total on the outing.

Cost and Hours: £15.50, includes 1.5-hour audioguide, daily 9:30-16:30, Oct until 16:00, Nov-March 10:00-15:30, these are last-entry times, tearoom; at the Ocean Terminal Shopping Mall, on Ocean Drive in Leith; tel. 0131/555-5566, www.royalyachtbritannia.co.uk.

Getting There: From central Edinburgh, catch Lothian bus #11 or #22 from Princes Street (just above Waverley Station), or #35 from the bottom of the Royal Mile (alongside the parliament building) to Ocean Terminal (last stop). From the B&B neighborhood, you can either bus to the city center and transfer to one of the buses above, or take bus #14 from Dalkeith Road to Mill Lane, then walk about 10 minutes. The Majestic Tour hop-on, hop-off bus stops here as well. Drivers can park free in the blue parking garage. Take the shopping center elevator to level E, then follow the signs.

Visiting the Ship: First, explore the **museum,** filled with engrossing royal-family-afloat history. You'll see lots of family photos that evoke the fine times the Windsors enjoyed on the *Britannia*, as well as some nautical equipment and uniforms. Then, armed with your audioguide, you're welcome aboard.

This was the last in a line of royal yachts that stretches back to 1660. With all its royal functions, the ship required a crew of more than 200. Begin in the captain's bridge, which feels like it's been preserved from the day it was launched in 1953. Then head down a deck to see the officers' quarters, then the garage, where a Rolls Royce was hoisted aboard to use in places where the local transportation wasn't up to royal standards. The Veranda Deck at the back of the ship was the favorite place for outdoor entertainment. Ronald Reagan, Boris Yeltsin, Bill Clinton, and Nelson Mandela all sipped champagne here. The Sun Lounge, just off the back Veranda Deck, was the Queen's favorite, with Burmese teak and the same phone system she was used to in Buckingham Palace. When she wasn't entertaining, the Queen liked it quiet. The crew wore sneakers, communicated in hand signals, and (at least near the Queen's quarters) had to be finished with all their work by 8:00 in the morning.

Take a peek into the adjoining his-and-hers bedrooms of the Queen and the Duke of Edinburgh (check out the spartan twin beds), and the honeymoon suite where Prince Charles and Lady Di began their wedded bliss.

Heading down another deck, walk through the officers' lounge (and learn about the rowdy games they played) and past the galleys (including custom cabinetry for the fine china and silver) on your way to the biggest room on the yacht, the state dining room. Now decorated with gifts given by the ship's many noteworthy guests, this space enabled the Queen to entertain a good-size crowd. The drawing room, while rather simple (the Queen

specifically requested "country house comfort"), was perfect for casual relaxing among royals. Princess Diana played the piano, which is bolted to the deck. Note the contrast to the decidedly less plush crew's quarters, mail room, sick bay, laundry, and engine room.

▲Rosslyn Chapel

This small but fascinating countryside church, about a 20-minute drive outside Edinburgh, is a riot of carved iconography. The patterned ceiling and walls have left scholars guessing about the symbolism for centuries.

Cost and Hours: £9, Mon-Sat 9:30-17:00, June-Aug until 18:00, Sun 12:00-16:45 year-round, located in Roslin Village, tel. 0131/440-2159, www.rosslynchapel.org.uk.

Getting There: Ride Lothian bus #37 from Princes Street (stop PJ), North Bridge, or Newington Road in the B&B neighborhood (1-2/hour, 45 minutes). By car, take the A-701 to Penicuik/Peebles, and follow signs for *Roslin;* once you're in the village, you'll see signs for the chapel.

Background: After it was featured in the climax of Dan Brown's 2003 bestseller *The Da Vinci Code,* the number of visitors to Rosslyn Chapel more than quadrupled. But the chapel's allure existed well before the books, and will endure long after they move from bargain bin to landfill. Founded in 1446 as the private mausoleum of the St. Clair family—who wanted to be buried close to God—the church's interior is carved with a stunning mishmash of Christian, pagan, family, Templar, Masonic, and other symbolism. After the Scottish Reformation, Catholic churches like this fell into disrepair. But in the 18th and 19th centuries, Romantics such as Robert Burns and Sir Walter Scott discovered these evocative old ruins, putting Rosslyn Chapel back on the map. Even Queen

Victoria visited, and gently suggested that the chapel be restored to its original state. Today, after more than a century of refits and refurbishments, the chapel transports visitors back to a distant and mysterious age.

Visiting the Chapel: From the ticket desk and visitors center, head

to the chapel itself. Ask about docent lectures (usually at the top of the hour). If you have time to kill, pick up the good laminated descriptions for a clockwise tour of the carvings. In the crypt—where the stonemasons worked—you can see faint architectural drawings engraved in the wall, used to help them plot out their master design.

Elsewhere, look for these fun details: In the corner to the left of the altar, find the angels playing instruments—including one with bagpipes. Nearby, you'll see a person dancing with a skeleton. This "dance of death" theme—common in the Middle Ages—is a reminder of mortality: We'll all die eventually, so we might as well whoop it up while we're here. On the other side of the nave are carvings of the seven deadly sins and the seven acts of mercy. One inscription reads: "Wine is strong. Kings are stronger. Women are stronger still. But truth conquers all."

Flanking the altar are two carved columns that come with a legend: The more standard-issue column, on the left, was executed by a master mason, who soon after (perhaps disappointed in his lack of originality) went on a sabbatical to gain inspiration. While he was gone, his ambitious apprentice carved the beautiful corkscrew-shaped column on the right. Upon returning, the master flew into an envious rage and murdered the apprentice with his carving hammer.

Scattered throughout the church, you'll also see the family's symbol, the "engrailed cross" (with serrated edges). Keep an eye out for the more than one hundred "green men"—chubby faces with leaves and vines growing out of their orifices, symbolizing nature. This paradise/Garden of Eden theme is enhanced by a smattering of exotic animals (monkey, elephant, camel, dragon, and a lion fighting a unicorn) and some exotic foliage: aloe vera, trillium, and corn. That last one (framing a window to the right of the altar) is a mystery: It was carved well before Columbus sailed the ocean blue, at a time when corn was unknown in Europe. Several theories have been suggested—some far-fetched (the father of the man who built the chapel explored the New World before Columbus), and others more plausible (the St. Clairs were of Norse descent, and the Vikings are known to have traveled to the Americas well before Columbus). Others simply say it's not corn at all—it's stalks of wheat. After all these centuries, Rosslyn Chapel's mysteries still inspire the imaginations of historians, novelists, and tourists alike.

Royal Botanic Garden

Britain's second-oldest botanical garden (after Oxford) was established in 1670 for medicinal herbs, and this 70-acre refuge is now one of Europe's best. A visitors center has temporary exhibits.

Cost and Hours: Gardens-free, greenhouse-£6.50, daily

10:00-18:00, Feb and Oct until 17:00, Nov-Jan until 16:00, greenhouse last entry one hour before closing, café and restaurant, a mile north of the city center at Inverleith Row, tel. 0131/248-2909, www.rbge.org.uk.

Getting There: It's a 10-minute bus ride from the city center: Take bus #8 from North Bridge, or #23 or #27 from George IV Bridge (near the National Museum) or The Mound. The Majestic Tour hop-on, hop-off bus also stops here.

Scottish National Gallery of Modern Art

This museum, set in a beautiful parkland, houses Scottish and international paintings and sculpture from 1900 to the present, including works by Matisse, Duchamp, Picasso, and Warhol. The grounds include a pleasant outdoor sculpture park and a café.

Cost and Hours: Free, daily 10:00-17:00, 75 Belford Road, tel. 0131/624-6336, www.nationalgalleries.org.

Getting There: It's about a 20-minute walk west from the city center. Or take the shuttle bus, which runs about hourly between this museum and the Scottish National Gallery (£1 donation requested, confirm times on website).

Experiences in Edinburgh

URBAN HIKES

▲▲Holyrood Park: Arthur's Seat and the Salisbury Crags

Rising up from the heart of Edinburgh, Holyrood Park is a lush green mountain squeezed between the parliament/Holyroodhouse (at the bottom of the Royal Mile) and my recommended B&B neighborhood. For an exhilarating hike, connect these two zones with a moderately strenuous 30-minute walk along the Salisbury Crags—reddish cliffs with sweeping views over the city. Or, for a more serious climb, make the ascent to the summit of Arthur's Seat, the 822-foot-tall remains of an extinct volcano. You can run up like they did in *Chariots of Fire*, or just stroll—at the summit, you'll be rewarded with commanding views of the town and surroundings. On May Day, be on the summit at dawn and wash your face in the morning dew to commemorate the Celtic holiday of Beltane, the celebration of spring. (Morning dew is supposedly very good for your complexion.)

You can do this hike either from the bottom of the Royal Mile, or from the B&B neighborhood.

From the Royal Mile: Begin in the parking lot below the Palace of Holyroodhouse. Facing the cliff, you'll see two trailheads. For the easier hike along the base of the **Salisbury Crags,** take the trail to the right. At the far end, you can descend into the Dalkeith Road area or—if you're up for more hiking—continue steeply up the switchbacked trail to the Arthur's Seat summit. If you know you'll want to ascend **Arthur's Seat** from the start, take the wider path on the left from the Holyroodhouse parking lot (easier grade, through the abbey ruins and "Hunter's Bog").

From the B&B Neighborhood: If you're sleeping in this area, enjoy a pre-breakfast or late-evening hike starting from the other side (in June, the sun comes up early, and it stays light until nearly midnight). From the Commonwealth Pool, take Holyrood Park Road, bear left at the first roundabout, then turn right at the second roundabout (onto Queen's Drive). Soon you'll see the trailhead, and make your choice: Bear right up the steeper "Piper's Walk" to **Arthur's**  **Seat** (about a 20-minute hike from here, up a steeply switchbacked trail), or bear left for an easier ascent up the "Radial Road" to the **Salisbury Crags,** which you can follow—with great views over town—all the way to Holyroodhouse Palace.

By Car: If you have a car, you can drive up most of the way to Arthur's Seat from behind (follow the one-way street from the palace, park safely and for free by the little lake, and hike up).

Duddingston Village and Dr. Neil's Garden

This low-key, 30-minute walk goes from the B&B neighborhood to Duddingston Village—a former village that got absorbed by the city but still retains its old, cobbled feel, local church, and great old-time pub, the recommended Sheep Heid Inn. Also here is Dr. Neil's Garden, a peaceful, free garden on a loch.

Walk behind the Commonwealth Pool along Holyrood Park Road. Before the roundabout, just after passing through the wall/gate, take the path to your right. This path runs alongside the Duddingston Low Road all the way to the village and garden. Ignore the road traffic and enjoy the views of Arthur's Seat, the golf course, and eventually, Duddingston Loch. When you reach the cobbled road, you're in Duddingston Village, with the church on your right and the Sheep Heid Inn a block down on your left. Another 100 feet down the main road is a gate labeled "*The Manse*" with the number 5—enter here for the garden.

Dr. Neil's Garden (also known as the Secret Garden) was started by doctors Nancy and Andrew Neil, who traveled throughout Europe in the 1960s gathering trees and plants. They brought them back here, planted them on this land, and tended to them with the help of their patients. Today it offers a quiet, secluded break from the city, where you can walk among flowers and trees and over quaint bridges, get inspired by quotes written on chalkboards, or sit on a bench overlooking the loch (free, daily 10:00-dusk, mobile 07849-187-995, www.drneilsgarden.co.uk).

▲Calton Hill

For an easy walk for fine views over all of Edinburgh, head up to Calton Hill—the monument-studded bluff that rises up from the eastern end of the New Town. From the Waverley Station area, simply head east on Princes Street (which becomes Waterloo Place).

About five minutes after passing North Bridge, watch on the right for the gated entrance to the **Old Calton Cemetery**—worth a quick walk-through for its stirring monuments to great Scots. The can't-miss-it round monument honors the philosopher David Hume; just next to that is a memorial topped by Abraham Lincoln, honoring Scottish-American troops who were killed in combat. The obelisk honors political martyrs.

The views from the cemetery are good, but for even better ones, head back out to the main road and continue a few more minutes

on Waterloo Place. Across the street, steps lead up into **Calton Hill.** Explore. Informational plaques identify the key landmarks. At the summit of the hill is the giant, unfinished replica of the Parthenon, honoring those lost in the Napoleonic Wars. Donations to finish it never materialized, leaving it with the nickname "Edinburgh's Disgrace." Nearby, the old observatory is filled with an avant-garde art gallery, and the back of the hillside boasts sweeping views over the Firth of Forth and Edinburgh's sprawl. Back toward the Old Town, the tallest tower celebrates Admiral Horatio Nelson—the same honoree of the giant pillar on London's Trafalgar Square. The best views are around the smaller, circular Dugald Stewart Monument, with postcard panoramas overlooking the spires of the Old Town and the New Town.

More Hikes

You can hike along the river (called the Water of Leith) through Edinburgh. Locals favor the stretch between Roseburn and Dean Village, but the 1.5-mile walk from Dean Village to the Royal Botanic Garden is also good. For more information on these and other hikes, ask at the TI or your B&B.

WHISKY AND GIN TASTING
Whisky Tasting

One of the most accessible places to learn about whisky is at the **Scotch Whisky Experience** on the Royal Mile, an expensive but informative overview to whisky, including a tasting (see page 55). To get more into sampling whisky, try one of the early-evening tastings at the recommended **Cadenhead's Whisky Shop** (see page 89).

Serious whisky drinkers can check out **The Scotch Malt Whisky Society** in the New Town. Formerly a private club, it recently opened the Kaleidoscope bar to the public, serving glasses from anonymous, numbered bottles of single malts from all over Scotland and beyond. In this "blind tasting" approach, you have to read each number's tasting notes to make your choice...or enlist the help of the bartender, who will probe you on what kind of flavor profile you like. While this place's shrouded-in-mystery pretense could get lost on novices, aficionados enjoy it (daily 11:00-23:00, bar serves light dishes, on-site restaurant, 28 Queen Street, tel. 0131/220-2044, www.smws.com).

Gin Distillery Tours

The residents of Edinburgh drink more gin per person than any other city in the United Kingdom, and the city is largely responsible for the recent renaissance of this drink, so it's only appropriate that you visit a gin distillery while in town. Two distilleries right in the heart of Edinburgh offer hour-long tours with colorful guides who discuss the history of gin, show you the stills involved in the production process, and ply you with libations. Both tours are popular and fill up; book ahead on their websites.

Pickering's is located in a former vet school and animal hospital at Summerhall, halfway between the Royal Mile and the B&B neighborhood—you'll still see cages lining the walls (£10, 3/day Thu-Sun, meet at the Royal Dick Bar in the central courtyard at 1 Summerhall, tel. 0131/290-2901, www.pickeringsgin.com).

Edinburgh Gin is in the New Town, next to the Waldorf Astoria Hotel. Besides the basic tour, there's a connoisseur tour with more tastings and a gin-making tour (basic tour £10, 3/day daily, 1A Rutland Place, tel. 0131/656-2810, www.edinburghgin.com). If you can't get on to one of their tours, visit their Heads & Tales bar to taste their gins (daily 17:00-24:00).

LEISURE ACTIVITIES

Several enjoyable activities cluster near the B&B area around Dalkeith Road. For details, check their websites.

The **Royal Commonwealth Pool** is an indoor fitness and activity complex with a 50-meter pool, gym/fitness studio, and kids' soft play zone (daily, tel. 0131/667-7211, www.edinburghleisure. co.uk).

The **Prestonfield Golf Club,** also an easy walk from the B&Bs, has golfers feeling like they're in a country estate (dress code, 6 Priestfield Road North, tel. 0131/667-9665, www.prestonfieldgolf. co.uk).

Farther out at **Midlothian Snowsports Centre** (a little south of town in Hillend; better for drivers), try skiing without any pesky snow. It feels like snow-skiing on a slushy day, even though you're schussing over matting misted with water. Four new tubing runs offer fun even for nonskiers (Mon-Fri 9:30-21:00, Sat-Sun until 19:00, tel. 0131/445-4433, http://ski.midlothian.gov.uk).

EDINBURGH'S FESTIVALS

Every summer, Edinburgh's annual festivals turn the city into a carnival of the arts. The season begins in June with the international film festival (www.edfilmfest.org.uk); then the jazz and blues festival in July (www.edinburghjazzfestival. com).

In August a riot of over-lapping festivals known collectively as the **Edinburgh Festival** rages simultaneously—international, fringe, book, and art, as well as the Military Tattoo. There are enough music, dance, drama, and multicultural events to make even the most jaded traveler giddy with excitement. Every day is jammed with formal and spontaneous fun. Many city sights run on extended hours. It's a glorious time to be in Edinburgh...*if* you have (and can afford) a room.

If you'll be in town in August, book your room and tickets for major events (especially the Tattoo) as far ahead as you can lock in dates. Plan carefully to ensure you'll have time for festival activities as well as sightseeing. Check online to confirm dates; the best overall website is www.edinburghfestivals.co.uk. Several publications—including the festival's official schedule, the *Edinburgh Festivals Guide Daily, The List, Fringe Program,* and *Daily Diary*—list and evaluate festival events.

The official, more formal **Edinburgh International Festival** is the original. Major events sell out well in advance (ticket office at the Hub, in the former Tolbooth Church near the top of the Royal Mile, tel. 0131/473-2000, www.hubtickets.co.uk or www. eif.co.uk).

The less formal **Fringe Festival,** featuring edgy comedy and theater, is huge—with 2,000 shows—and has eclipsed the original festival in popularity (ticket/info office just below St. Giles' Cathedral on the Royal Mile, 180 High Street, bookings tel. 0131/226-0000, www.edfringe.com). Tickets may be available at the door, and half-price tickets for some events are sold on the day of the show at the Half-Price Hut, located at The Mound, near the Scottish National Gallery.

The **Military Tattoo** is a massing of bands, drums, and bagpipes, with groups from all over the former British Empire and beyond. Displaying military finesse with a stirring lone-piper finale, this grand spectacle fills the Castle Esplanade (nightly during most of Aug except Sun, performances Mon-Fri at 21:00, Sat at 19:30 and 22:30, £25-63, booking starts in Dec, Fri-Sat shows sell out first, all seats generally sold out by early summer, some scattered same-day tickets may be available; office open Mon-Fri 10:00-16:30, closed Sat-Sun, during Tattoo open until show time and closed Sun; 32 Market Street, behind Waverley Station, tel. 0131/225-1188, www.edintattoo.co.uk). Some performances are filmed by the BBC and later broadcast as a big national television special.

The **Festival of Politics,** adding yet another dimension to Edinburgh's festival action, is held in August in the Scottish parliament building. It's a busy weekend of discussions and lectures on environmentalism, globalization, terrorism, gender, and other issues (www.festivalofpolitics.org.uk).

Other summer festivals cover books (mid-late Aug, www.edbookfest.co.uk) and art (late July-Aug, www.edinburghartfestival.com).

Shopping in Edinburgh

Edinburgh is bursting with Scottish clichés for sale: kilts, shortbread, whisky...if they can slap a tartan on it, they'll sell it. Locals dismiss the touristy trinket shops, which are most concentrated along the Royal Mile, as "tartan tat." Your challenge is finding something a wee bit more authentic. If you want to be sure you are taking home local merchandise, check if the labels read: "Made in Scotland." "Designed in Scotland" actually means "Made in China." Shops are usually open around 10:00-18:00 (later on Thu, shorter hours or closed on Sun). Tourist shops are open longer hours.

SHOPPING STREETS AND NEIGHBORHOODS
Near the Royal Mile: The Royal Mile is intensely touristy, mostly lined with interchangeable shops selling made-in-China souvenirs. I've listed a few worthwhile spots along here later, under "What to

Shop For." But in general, the area near Grassmarket, an easy stroll from the top of the Royal Mile, offer more originality. **Victoria Street,** which climbs steeply downhill from the Royal Mile (near the Hub/Tolbooth Church) to Grassmarket, has a fine concentration of local chain shops, including I.J. Mellis Cheesemonger and Walker Slater for designer tweed (both described later), plus Calzeat (scarves, throws, and other textiles), a Harry Potter store, and more clothing and accessory shops. **Candlemaker Row,** exiting Grassmarket opposite Victoria Street, is a little more artisan, with boutiques selling hats (everything from dapper men's caps to outrageous fascinators), jewelry, art, design items, and even fossils. The street winds a couple of blocks up toward the National Museum; Greyfriars Bobby awaits you at the top of the street (see page 70).

EDINBURGH

In New Town: For mass-market shopping, you'll find plenty of big chain stores along **Princes Street.** In addition to Marks & Spencer, H&M, Zara, Primark, and a glitzy Apple Store, you'll also see the granddaddy of Scottish department stores, Jenners (generally daily 9:30-18:30, open later on Thu, shorter hours on Sun; described on page 41). Parallel to Princes Street, **George Street** has higher-end chain stores (including many from London, such as L.K. Bennett, Molton Brown, and Karen Millen). Just off St. Andrew Square is a branch of the high-end London department store Harvey Nichols.

For more local, artisan shopping, check out **Thistle Street,** lined with some fun eateries and a good collection of shops. You'll see some fun boutiques selling jewelry, shoes, and clothing. This is also the home of Howie Nicolsby's 21st Century Kilts, which attempts to bring traditional Scottish menswear into the present day (described later).

WHAT TO SHOP FOR
Whisky
You can order whisky in just about any bar in town, and whisky shops are a dime a dozen around the Royal Mile. But the places I've listed here distinguish themselves by their tradition and helpful staff.

Cadenhead's Whisky Shop is not a tourist sight—don't expect free samples. Founded in 1842, this firm prides itself on bottling good whisky straight from casks at the distilleries, without all the compromises that come with

EDINBURGH

profitable mass production (coloring with sugar to fit the expected look, watering down to reduce the alcohol tax, and so on). Those drinking from Cadenhead-bottled whiskies will enjoy the pure product as the distilleries' owners themselves do, not as the sorry public does. The staff explains the sometimes-complex whisky board and talks you through flavor profiles. Buy the right bottle to enjoy in your hotel room night after night (prices start around £14 for about 7 ounces)—unlike wine, whisky has a long shelf life after it's opened. The bottles are extremely durable; ask them to demonstrate (Mon-Sat 10:30-17:30, closed Sun, 172 Canongate, tel. 0131/556-5864, www.wmcadenhead.com). They host hour-

EDINBURGH

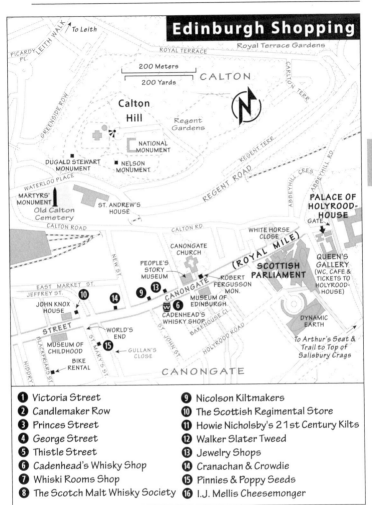

Edinburgh Shopping

1 Victoria Street
2 Candlemaker Row
3 Princes Street
4 George Street
5 Thistle Street
6 Cadenhead's Whisky Shop
7 Whiski Rooms Shop
8 The Scotch Malt Whisky Society
9 Nicolson Kiltmakers
10 The Scottish Regimental Store
11 Howie Nicholsby's 21st Century Kilts
12 Walker Slater Tweed
13 Jewelry Shops
14 Cranachan & Crowdie
15 Pinnies & Poppy Seeds
16 I.J. Mellis Cheesemonger

long whisky tastings during the week—a hit with aficionados (£25, Mon-Fri at 17:45, best to arrange in advance in peak season).

Whiski Rooms Shop, just off the Royal Mile, comes with a knowledgeable, friendly staff that happily assists novices and experts alike to select the right bottle. Their adjacent bar usually has about 400 open bottles: Serious purchasers can get a sample. Even better, try one of their tastings. You have two options: You can order a flight in the bar, which comes with written information about each whisky you're sampling (variety of options starting around £25, available anytime the bar is open). Or you can opt for a guided tasting (£22.50 introductory tasting, £40 premium tasting with the really good stuff, chocolate and cheese pairings also available; takes about one hour, reserve ahead). If you're doing a flight or a tasting, you'll get a small discount voucher for buying a bottle in the store (shop open daily 10:00-18:00, bar until 24:00, both open later in Aug, 4 North Bank Street, tel. 0131/225-1532, www. whiskirooms.com).

Near the B&B Neighborhood: Perhaps the most accessible place to learn about local whiskies is conveniently located in the B&B area south of the city center. **Wood-Winters** has a passion both for traditional  spirits and for the latest innovations in Edinburgh's booze scene. It's well stocked with 300 whiskies and gins (a trendy alternative to Scotch), as well as wines and local craft beers. Manager Rob invites curious browsers to sample a wee dram; he loves to introduce customers to something new (Mon-Tue 10:00-19:00, Wed-Sat until 21:00, Sun 13:00-17:00, 91 Newington Road, www.woodwinters.com, tel. 0131/667-2760). For location, see the map on page 99.

Kilts and Other Traditional Scottish Gear

Many of the kilt outfitters you'll see along the Royal Mile are selling cheap knock-offs, made with printed rather than woven tartan material. If you want a serious kilt—or would enjoy window-shopping for one—try one of the places below. These have a few off-the-rack options, but to get a kilt in your specific tartan and size, they'll probably take your measurements, custom-make it, and ship it to you. For a good-quality outfit (kilt, jacket, and accessories), plan on spending in the neighborhood of £1,000.

Nicolson Kiltmakers has a respect for tradition and quality. Owner Gordon enlists and trains local craftspeople who specialize in traditionally manufactured kilts and accessories. He prides himself on keeping the old ways alive (in the face of deeply discounted "tartan tat") and actively cultivates the next generation of kiltmakers (daily 9:30-17:30, 189 Canongate, tel. 0131/558-2887, www. nicolsonkiltmakers.co.uk).

The Scottish Regimental Store, run by Nigel, is the official outfitter for military regiments. They sell top-of-the-line, formal kiltwear, as well as medals and pins that can be a more affordable souvenir (Mon-Thu 10:00-16:00, Fri-Sat until 17:00, closed Sun,

9 Jeffrey Street, tel. 0131/557-0249, www.scottishregimentalstore. co.uk).

Howie Nicholsby's 21st Century Kilts, in the New Town, brings this traditional craft into the present day. It's fun to peruse his photos of both kilted celebrities (from Alan Cumming to Vin Diesel) and wedding albums—which make you wish you were Scottish, engaged, and wealthy enough to hire Howie to outfit your bridal party (Howie asks that you make an appointment, though you're welcome to drop in if he happens to be there; closed Sun-Mon and Wed, 48 Thistle Street, send text to 07774-757-222, www.21stcenturykilts.com, howie@21stcenturykilts.com).

EDINBURGH

Tweed

Several places around town sell the famous Harris Tweed (the authentic stuff is handwoven on the Isle of Harris). **Walker Slater** is the place to go for top-quality tweed at top prices. They have three locations on Victoria Street, just below the Royal Mile near Grassmarket: menswear (at #16), womenswear (#44), and a sale shop (#5). You'll find a rich interior and a wide variety of gorgeous jackets, scarves, bags, and more. This place feels elegant and exclusive (Mon-Sat 10:00-18:00, Sun 11:00-17:00, www.walkerslater.com).

Jewelry

Jewelry with Celtic designs, mostly made from sterling silver, is a popular and affordable souvenir. While you'll see these sold around town, two convenient shops face each other near the bottom of the Royal Mile: **Hamilton and Young,** which has a line of *Outlander*-inspired designs (173 Canongate), and **Celtic Design** (156 Canongate).

Food and Treats

Cranachan & Crowdie collects products (mostly edibles, some crafts) from more than 200 small, independent producers all over Scotland. The selection goes well beyond the mass-produced clichés, and American Beth and Scottish Fiona love to explain the story behind each item. They also offer up Scottish gin samples upon request (daily 11:00-18:00, on the Royal Mile at 263 Canongate, tel. 07951/587-420).

Pinnies & Poppy Seeds is a small, artisan bakery selling handmade shortbread made fresh daily from local, organic ingredients. Besides traditional all-butter shortbread, they have a rotating selection of 35 other flavors including chocolate hazelnut, rose pistachio, and cardamom white chocolate. They can package it for you to take home (lasts a month). They also sell other Scottish-made treats, both their own and from other local artisans, such as their Ballantyne Toffee from an old family recipe, gourmet marsh-mallows, shortbread truffles, and scented candles to match their shortbread flavors (Mon-Sat 10:00-17:30, closed Sun and in Jan, 26 St Mary's Street, tel. 0131/261-7012, run by American Jennifer).

I.J. Mellis Cheesemonger, tucked down Victoria Street just off the top of the Royal Mile, stocks a wide variety of Scottish, English, and international cheeses. They're as knowledgeable about cheese as they are generous with samples (Mon-Sat 9:30-19:00, Sun 11:00-18:00, 30A Victoria Street, tel. 0131/226-6215).

Nightlife in Edinburgh

▲▲Literary Pub Tour

This two-hour walk is interesting even if you think Sir Walter Scott won an Oscar for playing General Patton. You'll follow the witty dialogue of two actors as they debate whether the great literature of Scotland was high art or the creative re-creation of fun-loving louts fueled by a passion for whisky. You'll wander from the Grassmarket over the Old Town and New Town, with stops in three pubs, as your guides share their takes on Scotland's literary greats. The tour meets at the Beehive Inn on Grassmarket (£14, book online and save £2, May-Sept nightly at 19:30, April and Oct Thu-Sun, Jan-March Fri and Sun, Nov-Dec Fri only, tel. 0800-169-7410, www.edinburghliterarypubtour.co.uk).

▲Ghost Walks

A variety of companies lead spooky walks around town, provid-ing an entertaining and affordable night out (offered nightly, most around 19:00 and 21:00, easy socializing for solo travelers). These two options are the most established.

The theatrical and creatively staged **The Cadies & Witchery Tours,** the most established outfit, offers two different 1.25-hour walks: "Ghosts and Gore" (April-Aug only, in daylight and follow-ing a flatter route) and "Murder and Mystery" (year-round, after dark, hillier, more surprises and scares). The cost for either tour is the same (£10, includes book of stories, leaves from top of Royal Mile, outside the Witchery Restaurant, near Castle Esplanade, res-ervations required, tel. 0131/225-6745, www.witcherytours.com).

Auld Reekie Tours offers a scary array of walks daily and nightly (£12-16, 60-90 minutes, leaves from front steps of the Tron Church building on Cockburn Street, tel. 0131/557-4700, www.auldreekietours.com). Auld Reekie focuses on the paranormal, witch covens, and pagan temples, taking groups into the "haunted vaults" under the old bridges "where it was so dark, so crowded, and so squalid that the people there knew each other not by how they looked, but by how they sounded, felt, and smelt." If you want more, there's plenty of it (complete with screaming Gothic "jumpers").

Scottish Folk Evenings

A variety of £35-40 dinner shows, generally for tour groups intent on photographing old cultural clichés, are held in the huge halls of expensive hotels. (Prices are bloated to include 20 percent commissions.) Your "traditional" meal is followed by a full slate of swirling kilts, blaring bagpipes, and Scottish folk dancing with an old-time music hall emcee. If you like Lawrence Welk, you're in for a treat. But for most travelers, these are painfully cheesy. You can sometimes see the show without dinner for about two-thirds the price. The TI has fliers on all the latest venues.

Prestonfield House, a luxurious venue near the Dalkeith Road B&Bs, offers its kitschy "Taste of Scotland" folk evening with or without dinner Sunday to Friday. For £50, you get the show with two drinks and a wad of haggis; £65 buys you the same, plus a three-course meal and a half-bottle of wine (be there at 18:45, dinner at 19:00, show runs 20:00-22:00, April-Oct only). It's in the stables of "the handsomest house in Edinburgh," which is now home to the recommended Rhubarb Restaurant (Priestfield Road, a 10-minute walk from Dalkeith Road B&Bs, tel. 0131/225-7800, www.scottishshow.co.uk).

For something more lowbrow—and arguably more authentic—in summer, you can watch the **Princes Street Gardens Dancers** perform a range of Scottish country dancing. The volunteer troupe will demonstrate each dance, then invite spectators to give it a try (£5, June-July Mon 19:30-21:30, at Ross Bandstand in Princes Street Gardens—in the glen just below Edinburgh Castle, tel. 0131/228-8616, www.princesstreetgardensdancing.org.uk). The same group offers summer programs in other parts of town (see website for details).

Theater

Even outside festival time, Edinburgh is a fine place for lively and affordable theater. Pick up *The List* for a complete rundown of what's on (free at TI; also online at www.list.co.uk).

▲▲Live Music in Pubs

While traditional music venues have been eclipsed by beer-focused student bars, Edinburgh still has a few good pubs that can deliver a traditional folk-music fix. The monthly *Gig Guide* (free at TI, accommodations, and various pubs, www.gigguide.co.uk) lists several places each night that have live music, divided by genre (pop, rock, world, and folk).

South of the Royal Mile: Sandy Bell's is a tight little pub with live folk music nightly from 21:30 (near National Museum of Scotland at 25 Forrest Road, tel. 0131/225-2751). Food is very simple (toasted sandwiches and pies), drinks are cheap, tables are small, and the vibe is local. They also have a few sessions earlier in the day (Sat at 14:00, Sun at 16:00, Mon at 17:30).

Captain's Bar is a cozy, music-focused pub with live sessions of folk and traditional music nightly around 21:00—see website for lineup (4 South College Street, http://captainsedinburgh.webs.com).

The Royal Oak is another good—if small—place for a dose of folk and blues (just off South Bridge opposite Chambers Road at 1 Infirmary Street, tel. 0131/557-2976).

The **Grassmarket** neighborhood (below the castle) bustles with live music and rowdy people spilling out of the pubs and into what was (once upon a time) a busy market square. While it used to be a mecca for Scottish folk music, today it's more youthful with a heavy-drinking, rockin' feel. It's fun to just wander through this area late at night and check out the scene. Thanks to the music and crowds, you'll know where to go...and where not to. Have a beer and follow your ear to places like **Biddy Mulligans** or **White Hart Inn** (both on Grassmarket). **Finnegans Wake,** on Victoria Street (which leads down to Grassmarket), also has live music in a variety of genres each night.

On the Royal Mile: Three characteristic pubs within a few steps of each other on High Street (opposite Radisson Hotel) offer a fun setting, classic pub architecture and ambience, and live music for the cost of a beer: **Whiski Bar** (mostly trad and folk; nightly at 22:00), **Royal Mile** (variety of genres; nightly at 22:00), and **Mitre Bar** (acoustic pop/rock with some trad; Fri-Sun at 21:30).

Just a block away (on South Bridge) is **Whistlebinkies Live Music Bar.** While they rarely do folk or Scottish trad, this is the most serious of the music pubs, with an actual stage and several acts nightly (schedule posted inside the door makes the genre clear; most nights music starts at 19:00 or 21:30, young crowd, fun energy, sticky floors, no cover, tel. 0131/557-5114). **No. 1 High Street** is an accessible little pub with a love of folk and traditional music (Wed-Thu from about 21:00, 1 High Street, tel. 0131/556-5758). **World's End,** across the street, also has music starting about 21:00 (trad on Thu, other genres Fri-Sat, 4 High Street, tel. 0131/556-3628).

In the New Town: All the beer drinkers seem to head for the pedestrianized Rose Street, famous for having the most pubs per square inch anywhere in Scotland—and plenty of live music.

Pubs near the B&B Neighborhood

The pubs in the B&B area don't typically have live music, but some are fun evening hangouts. **Leslie's Bar,** sitting between a working-class and an upper-class neighborhood, has two sides. Originally, the gang would go in on the right to gather around the great hardwood bar, glittering with a century of *Cheers* ambience. Meanwhile, the more delicate folks would slip in on the left, with its discreet doors, plush snugs (cozy private booths), and ornate ordering windows. Since 1896, this Victorian classic has been appreciated for both its real ales and its huge selection of fine whiskies (listed on a lengthy menu). Dive into the whisky mosh pit on the right, and let them show you how whisky can become "a very good friend." (daily 12:00-24:00, 49 Ratcliffe Terrace, tel. 0131/667-7205.)

Other good pubs in this area include **The Old Bell** (uphill from Leslie's, popular and cozy, with big TV screens) and **The Salisbury Arms** (bigger, more sprawling, feels upscale); both are described later, under "Eating in Edinburgh."

Sleeping in Edinburgh

To stay in the city center, you'll likely have to stay in a larger hotel or more impersonal guesthouse. For the classic B&B experience, look to the area south of town. A number of B&Bs cluster along Dalkeith Road and on side streets just off of it (south of the Royal Commonwealth Pool), and also along the parallel street Mayfield Gardens (which leads directly to South Bridge in the center). From either area, it's a long walk to the city center (about 25 minutes) or a quick bus or taxi/Uber ride.

While many of my B&B listings are not cheap (generally around £90-130), most come with friendly hosts and great cooked breakfasts. And they're generally cheaper than staying at a city-center hotel.

Note that during the Festival in August, prices skyrocket and most places do not accept bookings for one- or even two-night stays. If coming in August, book far in advance. Conventions, rugby matches, school holidays, and weekends can make finding a room tough at other times of year, too. In winter, when demand is light, some B&Bs close, and prices at all accommodations get soft.

For some travelers, short-term Airbnb-type rentals can be a good alternative to hotels; search for places in my recommended hotel and B&B neighborhoods. See page 121 for more information.

B&BS SOUTH OF THE CITY CENTER

At these not-quite-interchangeable places, character is provided by the personality quirks of the hosts and sometimes the decor. In

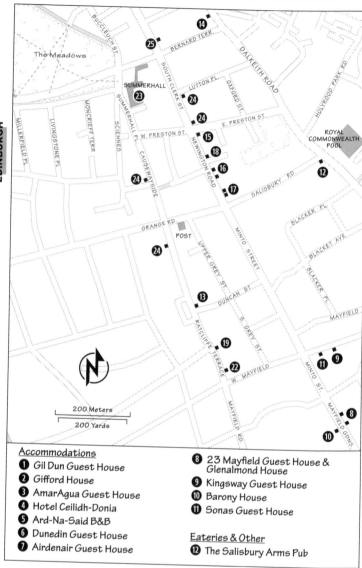

Accommodations

1. Gil Dun Guest House
2. Gifford House
3. AmarAgua Guest House
4. Hotel Ceilidh-Donia
5. Ard-Na-Said B&B
6. Dunedin Guest House
7. Airdenair Guest House
8. 23 Mayfield Guest House & Glenalmond House
9. Kingsway Guest House
10. Barony House
11. Sonas Guest House

Eateries & Other

12. The Salisbury Arms Pub

general, cash is preferred and can lead to discounted rates. Book direct—you will pay a much higher rate through a booking service.

Near the B&Bs, you'll find plenty of fine eateries (see "Eating in Edinburgh," later) and some good, classic pubs (see "Nightlife in Edinburgh," earlier). A few places have their own private parking; others offer access to easy, free street parking (ask when booking—or better yet, don't rent a car for your time in Edinburgh). The near-

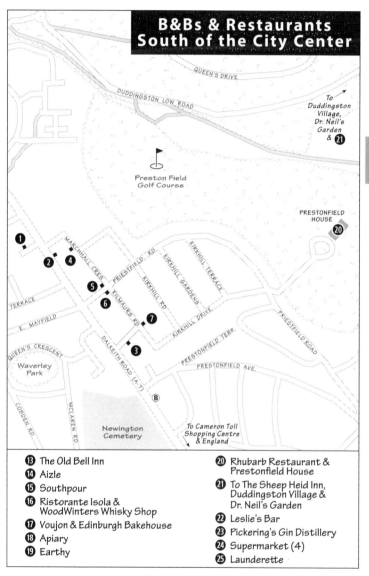

B&Bs & Restaurants South of the City Center

EDINBURGH

- ⑬ The Old Bell Inn
- ⑭ Aizle
- ⑮ Southpour
- ⑯ Ristorante Isola & WoodWinters Whisky Shop
- ⑰ Voujon & Edinburgh Bakehouse
- ⑱ Apiary
- ⑲ Earthy
- ⑳ Rhubarb Restaurant & Prestonfield House
- ㉑ To The Sheep Heid Inn, Duddingston Village & Dr. Neil's Garden
- ㉒ Leslie's Bar
- ㉓ Pickering's Gin Distillery
- ㉔ Supermarket (4)
- ㉕ Launderette

est launderette is Ace Cleaning Centre (which picks up and drops off; see page 15).

Taxi or Uber fare between the city center and the B&Bs is about £7. If taking the bus from the B&Bs into the city, hop off at the South Bridge stop for the Royal Mile (£1.60 single ride, £4 day ticket, use exact change; see the next page for more bus specifics).

Near Dalkeith Road

Most of my B&Bs near Dalkeith Road are located south of the Royal Commonwealth Pool. This comfortable, safe neighborhood is a ten-minute bus ride from the Royal Mile.

To get here from the train station, catch the bus around the corner on North Bridge: Exit the station onto Princes Street, turn right, cross the street, and walk up the bridge to the bus stop in front of the Marks & Spencer department store (#14, #30, or #33). About 10 minutes into the ride, after following South Clerk Street for a while, the bus makes a left turn, then a right. Depending on where you're staying, you'll get off at the first or second stop after the turn (confirm specifics with your B&B).

$$ Gil Dun Guest House, with eight rooms—some contemporary, others more traditional—is on a quiet cul-de-sac just off Dalkeith Road. It's comfortable, pleasant, and managed with care by Gerry and Bill; Maggie helps out and keeps things immaculate (family rooms, two-night minimum in summer preferred, limited off-street parking, 9 Spence Street, tel. 0131/667-1368, www.gildun.co.uk, gildun.edin@btinternet.com).

$$ Gifford House, on busy Dalkeith Road, is a bright, flowery retreat with six peaceful rooms (some with ornate cornices and views of Arthur's Seat) and compact, modern bathrooms (RS%, family rooms, cash preferred, street parking, 103 Dalkeith Road, tel. 0131/667-4688, www.giffordhouseedinburgh.com, giffordhouse@btinternet.com, David and Margaret).

$$ AmarAgua Guest House is an inviting Victorian home away from home, with five welcoming rooms, a Japanese garden, and eager hosts (one double has private bath down the hall, 2-night minimum, no kids under 12, street parking, 10 Kilmaurs Terrace, tel. 0131/667-6775, www.amaragua.co.uk, reservations@amaragua.co.uk, Lucia and Kuan).

$$ Hotel Ceilidh-Donia is bigger (17 rooms) and more hotel-like than other nearby B&Bs, with a bar and a small reception area, but managers Kevin and Susan and their staff provide a guesthouse warmth. The back deck is a pleasant place to sit on a warm day (family room, two-night minimum on peak-season weekends, 14 Marchhall Crescent, tel. 0131/667-2743, www.hotelceilidh-donia.co.uk, reservations@hotelceilidh-donia.co.uk).

$$ Ard-Na-Said B&B, in an elegant 1875 Victorian house, has seven bright, spacious rooms with modern bathrooms, including one ground-floor room with a pleasant patio (two-night minimum preferred in summer, off-street parking, 5 Priestfield Road, tel. 0131/283-6524, mobile 07476-606-202, www.ardnasaid.co.uk, info@ardnasaid.co.uk, Audrey Ballantine and her son Steven).

$$ Dunedin Guest House (dun-EE-din) is bright and plush, with seven well-decorated rooms, an angelic atrium, and a spacious breakfast room/lounge with TV (family rooms, one room with private bath down the hall, includes continental breakfast, extra charge for cooked breakfast, limited off-street parking, 8 Priestfield Road, tel. 0131/468-3339, www.dunedinguesthouse.co.uk, reservations@dunedinguesthouse.co.uk, Mary and Tony).

$ Airdenair Guest House is a hands-off guesthouse, with no formal host greeting (you'll get an access code to let yourself in) and a self-serve breakfast buffet. But the price is nice and the five simple rooms are well-maintained (29 Kilmaurs Road, tel. 0131/468-0173, http://airdenair-edinburgh.co.uk, contact@airdenair-edinburgh.co.uk, Duncan).

On or near Mayfield Gardens

These places are just a couple of blocks from the Dalkeith Road options, along the busy Newington Road (which turns in to Mayfield Gardens). All have private parking. To reach them from the center, hop on bus #3, #7, #8, #29, #31, #37, or #49. Note: Some of these buses depart from the second bus stop, a bit farther along North Bridge. To ride from these guesthouses to the city center, simply hop on any bus (except #47).

$$$ At 23 Mayfield Guest House, Ross and Kathleen (with their wee helpers Ethan and Alfie) rent seven splurge-worthy, thoughtfully appointed rooms complete with high-tech bathrooms (rain showers and motion-sensor light-up mirrors). Little extras—such as locally sourced gourmet breakfasts, an inviting guest lounge outfitted with leather-bound Sir Arthur Conan Doyle books, an "honesty bar," and classic black-and-white movie screenings—make you feel like royalty (RS% if you pay cash, family room for up to 4, two-night minimum preferred in summer, 23 Mayfield Gardens, tel. 0131/667-5806, www.23mayfield.co.uk, info@23mayfield.co.uk). They also rent an apartment (details on website).

$$$ Glenalmond House, run by Jimmy and Fiona Mackie, has nine elegantly decorated rooms featuring elaborately carved mahogany pieces (RS% if you pay cash, family room, no kids under 5, 25 Mayfield Gardens, tel. 0131/668-2392, www.glenalmondhouse.com, enquiries@glenalmondhouse.com).

$$ Kingsway Guest House, with seven stylish rooms, is owned by conscientious, delightful Gary and Lizzie, who have thought of all the little touches, such as a DVD library and in-room Internet radios, and offer good advice on neighborhood eats (RS% if you pay cash, family room, one room with private bath down the hall, 5 East Mayfield, tel. 0131/667-5029, www.edinburgh-guesthouse.com, booking@kingswayguesthouse.com).

$$ Barony House is run with infectious enthusiasm by Aussies Paul and Susan. Their eight doubles are each named and themed, and lovingly decorated by Susan, who's made the beautiful fabric headboards and created some of the art (she also bakes welcome pastries for guests). Two of the rooms are next door, in a former servants quarters, now a peaceful retreat with access to a shared kitchen (three-night minimum preferred in summer, no kids under 9, 20 Mayfield Gardens, tel. 0131/662-9938, www.baronyhouse.co.uk, booknow@baronyhouse.co.uk).

$$ Sonas Guest House is nothing fancy—just a simple, easy-going place with seven rooms, six of which have bathtubs (family room, 3 East Mayfield, tel. 0131/667-2781, www.sonasguesthouse.com, info@sonasguesthouse.com, Irene and Dennis).

HOTELS IN THE CITY CENTER

While a B&B generally provides more warmth, character, and lower prices, a city-center hotel gives you more walkability and access to sights and Edinburgh's excellent restaurant and pub scene. Prices are very high in peak season and drop substantially in off-season (a good time to shop around). In each case, I'd skip the institutional breakfast and eat out. You'll generally pay about £10 a day to park near these hotels.

$$$$ Macdonald Holyrood Hotel is a four-star splurge, with 157 rooms up the street from the parliament building and Holyroodhouse Palace. With its classy marble-and-wood decor, fitness center, spa, and pool, it's hard to leave. On a gray winter day in Edinburgh, this could be worth it (pricey breakfast, elevator, pay valet parking, near bottom of Royal Mile, across from Dynamic Earth, 81 Holyrood Road, tel. 0131/528-8000, www.macdonaldhotels.co.uk, newres@macdonald-hotels.co.uk).

$$$$ The Inn on the Mile is your trendy, central option, filling a renovated old bank building right in the heart of the Royal Mile (at North Bridge/South Bridge). The nine bright and stylish rooms are an afterthought to the busy upmarket pub, which is where you'll check in. If you don't mind some noise (from the pub and the busy street) and climbing lots of stairs, it's a handy home base (breakfast extra, complimentary drink, 82 High Street, tel. 0131/556-9940, www.theinnonthemile.co.uk, info@theinnonthemile.co.uk).

$$$$ The Inn Place, part of a small chain, fills the zformer headquarters of *The Scotsman* newspaper—a few steep steps below the Royal Mile—with 41 characterless, minimalist rooms ("bunk rooms" for 6-8 people, best deals on weekdays, breakfast extra, elevator, 20 Cockburn Street, tel. 0131/526-3780, www.

theinnplaceedinburgh.co.uk, reception@theinnplaceedinburgh.co.uk).

$$$ Grassmarket Hotel's 42 rooms are quirky and fun, from the Dandy comic-book wallpaper to the giant wall map of Edinburgh equipped with planning-your-visit magnets. The hotel is in a great location right on Grassmarket overlooking the Covenanters Memorial and above Biddy Mulligans Bar (family rooms, two-night minimum on weekends, elevator only serves half the rooms, 94 Grassmarket, tel. 0131/220-2299, www.grassmarkethotel.co.uk).

$$$ The Place Hotel, sister of the Inn Place listed earlier, has a fine New Town location 10 minutes north of the train station. It occupies three grand Georgian townhouses, with no elevator and long flights of stairs leading up to the 47 contemporary, no-frills rooms. Their outdoor terrace with retractable roof and heaters is a popular place to unwind (save money with a smaller city double, 34 York Place, tel. 0131/556-7575, www.yorkplace-edinburgh.co.uk, frontdesk@yorkplace-edinburgh.co.uk).

$$ Motel One Edinburgh Royal, part of a stylish German budget-hotel chain, is between the train station and the Royal Mile; it feels upscale and trendy for its price range (208 rooms, pay more for a park view or less for a windowless "budget" room with skylight, breakfast extra, elevator, 18 Market Street, tel. 0131/220-0730, www.motel-one.com, edinburgh-royal@motel-one.com; second location in the New Town/shopping zone at 10 Princes Street).

Chain Hotels in the Center: Besides my recommendations above, you'll find a number of cookie-cutter chain hotels close to the Royal Mile, including **Jurys Inn** (43 Jeffrey Street), **Ibis Hotel** (two convenient branches: near the Tron Church and another around the corner along the busy South Bridge), **Holiday Inn Express** (two locations: just off the Royal Mile at 300 Cowgate and one in the New Town), and **Travelodge Central** (just below the Royal Mile at 33 St. Mary's Street; additional locations in the New Town).

HOSTELS

¢ Baxter Hostel is your boutique hostel option. Occupying one floor of a Georgian townhouse (up several long, winding flights of stairs and below two more hostels), it has tons of ambience: tartan wallpaper, wood paneling, stone walls, decorative tile floors, and a beautifully restored kitchen/lounge that you'd want in your own house. Space is tight—hallways are snug, and five dorms (42 beds) share one bathroom. Another room, with four beds, has its own en-suite bathroom (includes scrambled-egg breakfast; small

1. Macdonald Holyrood Hotel
2. The Inn on the Mile
3. The Inn Place
4. Grassmarket Hotel
5. The Place Hotel
6. Motel One Edinburgh (2)
7. Baxter Hostel
8. To Edinburgh Central Youth Hostel
9. SafeStay Edinburgh Hostel
10. High Street Hostel
11. Royal Mile Backpackers Hostel
12. Castle Rock Hostel

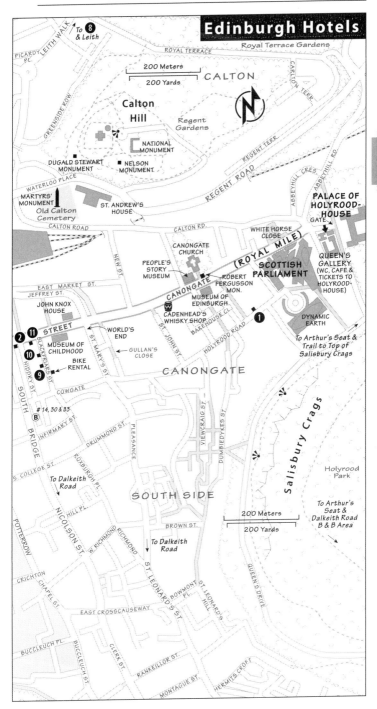

EDINBURGH

fee for towel, travel adapters, and locks; 5 West Register Street, tel. 0131/503-1001, www.thebaxter.eu, info@thebaxter.eu).

¢ **Edinburgh Central Youth Hostel** rents 251 beds in 72 rooms accommodating three to six people (all with private bathrooms and lockers). Guests can eat cheaply in the cafeteria, or cook for the cost of groceries in the members' kitchen (private rooms available, pay laundry, 15-minute downhill walk from Waverley Station—head down Leith Walk, pass through two roundabouts, hostel is on your left—or take Lothian bus #22 or #25 to Elm Rowe, 9 Haddington Place off Leith Walk, tel. 0131/524-2090, www.syha.org.uk, central@syha.org.uk).

¢ **SafeStay Edinburgh,** just off the Royal Mile, rents 272 bunks in pleasing purple-accented rooms. Dorm rooms have 4 to 12 beds, and there are also a few private singles and twin rooms (all rooms have private bathrooms). Bar 50 in the basement has an inviting lounge. Half of the rooms function as a university dorm during the school year, becoming available just in time for the tourists (breakfast extra, kitchen, laundry, free daily walking tour, 50 Blackfriars Street, tel. 0131/524-1989, www.safestay.com, reservations-edi@safestay.com).

¢ **Cheap and Scruffy Bohemian Hostels in the Center:** These three sister hostels—popular crash pads for young, hip backpackers—are beautifully located in the noisy center (some locations also have private rooms, www.macbackpackers.com): **High Street Hostel** (140 beds, 8 Blackfriars Street, just off High Street/Royal Mile, tel. 0131/557-3984); **Royal Mile Backpackers** (40 beds, 105 High Street, tel. 0131/557-6120); and **Castle Rock Hostel** (300 beds, just below the castle and above the pubs, 15 Johnston Terrace, tel. 0131/225-9666).

Eating in Edinburgh

Reservations for restaurants are essential in August and on weekends, and a good idea anytime. Children aren't allowed in many of the pubs.

THE OLD TOWN

Pricey places abound on the Royal Mile (listed later). While those are tempting, I prefer the two areas described first, each within a few minutes' walk of the Mile—just far enough to offer better value and a bit less touristy crush.

On Victoria Street, Near Grassmarket

$$$$ **Grainstore Restaurant,** a sedate and dressy world of wood, stone, and candles tucked away above busy Victoria Street, has served Scottish produce with a French twist for more than two

decades. While they have inexpensive £14 two-course lunch specials, dinner is à la carte. Reservations are recommended (daily 12:00-14:30 & 18:00-21:30, 30 Victoria Street, tel. 0131/225-7635, www.grainstore-restaurant.co.uk).

$$$ Maison Bleue Restaurant is popular for their à la carte French/Scottish/North African menu and dinner special before 18:30 (18:00 on Fri-Sat; open daily 12:00-22:00, 36 Victoria Street, tel. 0131/226-1900).

$ Oink carves from a freshly roasted pig each afternoon for sandwiches that come in "oink" or "grunter" sizes. Watch the pig shrink in the front window throughout the day (daily 11:00-18:00 or whenever they run out of meat, cash only, 34 Victoria Street, tel. 01890/761-355). There's another location at the bottom end of the Royal Mile, near the parliament building (at 82 Canongate).

Near the National Museum

These restaurants are happily removed from the Royal Mile melee and skew to a youthful clientele with few tourists. After passing the Greyfriars Bobby statue and the National Museum, fork left onto Forrest Road.

$ Union of Genius is a creative soup kitchen with a strong identity. They cook up a selection of delicious soups with fun foodie twists each morning at their main location in Leith, then deliver them to this shop by bicycle (for environmental reasons). These are supplemented with good salads and fresh-baked breads. The "flight" comes with three small cups of soup and three types of bread. Line up at the counter, then either take your soup to go or sit in the cramped interior, with a couple of tables and counter seating (Mon-Fri 10:00-16:00, Sat from 12:00, closed Sun, 8 Forrest Road, tel. 0131/226-4436).

$$ Mums is a kitschy diner serving up comfort food just like mum used to make. The menu runs to huge portions of heavy, greasy Scottish/British standards—bangers (sausages), meat pies, burgers, and artery-clogging breakfasts (served until 12:00)—all done with a foodie spin, including vegetarian options (Mon-Sat 9:00-22:00, Sun from 10:00, 4A Forrest Road, tel. 0131/260-9806).

$$ Ting Thai Caravan, just around the corner from the previous listings, is a casual, industrial-mod, food-focused eatery selling adventurous Thai street food (daily 11:30-22:00, Fri-Sat until 23:00, 8 Teviot Place, tel. 0131/225-9801).

Dessert: The **Frisky** frozen-yogurt shop, on Forrest Road, makes for a fun treat.

Along the Royal Mile

Though the eateries along this most-crowded stretch of the city are invariably touristy, the scene is fun. Sprinkled in this list are some

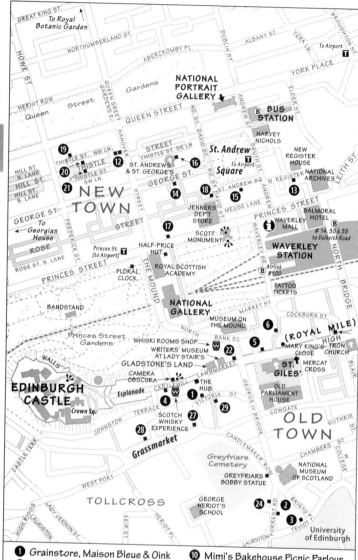

1 Grainstore, Maison Bleue & Oink
2 Union of Genius, Mums & Frisky
3 Ting Thai Caravan
4 The Witchery by the Castle
5 Angels with Bagpipes
6 Devil's Advocate
7 Wedgwood Restaurant
8 David Bann
9 Edinburgh Larder
10 Mimi's Bakehouse Picnic Parlour
11 Clarinda's Tea Room
12 Hendersons (3)
13 Café Royal
14 The Dome Restaurant
15 Dishoom
16 St. Andrew's & St. George's Church Undercroft Café
17 Marks & Spencer Food Hall
18 Sainsbury's

EDINBURGH

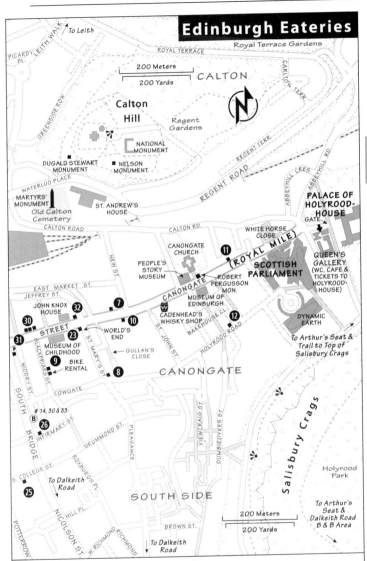

Edinburgh Eateries

To Leith

PICARDY PL.

LEITH WALK

GREENSIDE ROW

ROYAL TERRACE

Royal Terrace Gardens

CALTON

200 Meters

200 Yards

Calton Hill

Regent Gardens

NATIONAL MONUMENT

DUGALD STEWART MONUMENT

NELSON MONUMENT

WATERLOO PLACE

MARTYRS' MONUMENT

Old Calton Cemetery

ST. ANDREW'S HOUSE

REGENT TERR.

REGENT ROAD

ABBEYHILL CRES.

ABBEYHILL RD.

PALACE OF HOLYROODHOUSE

GATE

CALTON ROAD

CALTON RD.

WHITE HORSE CLOSE

CANONGATE CHURCH

PEOPLE'S STORY MUSEUM

ROBERT FERGUSSON MON.

① ②

ROYAL MILE

SCOTTISH PARLIAMENT

QUEEN'S GALLERY (WC, CAFE & TICKETS TO HOLYROODHOUSE)

EAST MARKET ST.

JEFFREY ST.

JOHN KNOX HOUSE

③②

⑦

CANONGATE

MUSEUM OF EDINBURGH

CADENHEAD'S WHISKY SHOP

⑩

⑫

BAKEHOUSE CL.

HOLYROOD ROAD

DYNAMIC EARTH

To Arthur's Seat & Trail to Top of Salisbury Crags

③⓪

③①

STREET

BLACKFRIARS ST.

②③

MUSEUM OF CHILDHOOD

⑨ BIKE RENTAL

WORLD'S END

ST. MARY'S ST.

ST. JOHN ST.

GULLAN'S CLOSE

⑧

CANONGATE

Salisbury Crags

NIDDRY ST.

COWGATE

SOUTH BRIDGE

Ⓑ #14, 30 & 33

②⑥

INFIRMARY ST.

DRUMMOND ST.

PLEASANCE

ROXBURGH PL.

VIEWCRAIG ST.

DUMBIEDYKES ST.

Holyrood Park

S. COLLEGE ST.

To Dalkeith Road

②⑤

POTTERROW

NICOLSON ST.

HILL PL.

W. RICHMOND

RICHMOND

SOUTH SIDE

BROWN ST.

To Dalkeith Road

200 Meters

200 Yards

To Arthur's Seat & Dalkeith Road B & B Area

⑲ Le Café St. Honoré

⑳ The Bon Vivant

㉑ El Cartel

Pubs & Nightlife

㉒ Deacon Brodie's Tavern

㉓ The World's End Pub

㉔ Sandy Bell's Pub

㉕ Captain's Bar

㉖ The Royal Oak Pub

㉗ Biddy Mulligans

㉘ White Hart Inn

㉙ Finnegans Wake

㉚ Whiski Bar, Royal Mile & Mitre Bar

㉛ Whistlebinkies Bar

㉜ No. 1 High Street Pub

places a block or two off the main drag offering better values and maybe fewer tourists.

Sit-Down Restaurants

These are listed roughly in downhill order, starting at the castle. You'll have more success getting into any of these with a reservation, especially on weekends.

$$$$ The Witchery by the Castle is set in a lushly decorated 16th-century building just below the castle on the Royal Mile, with wood paneling, antique candlesticks, tapestries, and opulent red-leather upholstery. Frequented by celebrities, tourists, and locals out for a splurge, the restaurant's emphasis is on pricey Scottish meats and seafood. Their Secret Garden dining room, in a separate building farther back, is also a special setting—down some steps and in a fanciful room with French doors opening on to a terrace. Reserve ahead for either space, dress smartly, and bear in mind you're paying a premium for the ambience (two-course lunch specials—also available before 17:30 and after 22:30, three-course dinner menu, daily 12:00-23:30, tel. 0131/225-5613, www.thewitchery.com).

$$$ Angels with Bagpipes, conveniently located across from St. Giles' Cathedral, serves sophisticated Scottish staples in its dark, serious, plush interior (two- and three-course lunches, tasting menus at dinner, daily 12:00-21:30, 343 High Street, tel. 0131/220-1111, www.angelswithbagpipes.co.uk).

$$$ Devil's Advocate is a popular gastropub that hides down the narrow lane called Advocates Close, directly across the Royal Mile from St. Giles'. With an old cellar setting—exposed stone and heavy beams—done up in modern style, it feels like a mix of old and new Edinburgh. Creative whisky cocktails kick off a menu that dares to be adventurous, but with a respect for Scottish tradition (daily 12:00-22:00, later for drinks, 8 Advocates Close, tel. 0131/225-4465).

$$$$ Wedgwood Restaurant is romantic, contemporary, chic, and as gourmet as possible with no pretense. Paul Wedgwood cooks while his wife Lisa serves with appetizing charm. The cuisine: creative, modern Scottish with an international twist and a whiff of Asia. The pigeon-and-haggis starter is scrumptious. Paul and Lisa believe in making the meal the event of the evening—don't come here to eat and run. I like the ground level with the Royal Mile view, but the busy kitchen ambience in the basement is also nice (fine wine by the glass, daily 12:00-15:00 & 18:00-22:00, reservations advised, 267 Canongate on Royal Mile, tel. 0131/558-8737, www.wedgwoodtherestaurant.co.uk).

$$$ David Bann is a worthwhile stop for well-heeled vegetarians in need of a break from the morning fry-up. While vegetarian as can be, this place doesn't have even a hint of hippie. It's upscale (it has a cocktail bar), sleek, minimalist, and stylish (gorgeously presented dishes), serious about quality, and organic. Reserve ahead (decadent desserts, Mon-Fri 12:00-22:00, Sat-Sun from 11:00, vegan and gluten-free options, just off the Royal Mile at 56 St. Mary's Street, tel. 0131/556-5888, www.davidbann.co.uk).

Quick, Easy, and Cheap Lunch Options

$ Edinburgh Larder promises "a taste of the country" in the center of the city. They focus on high-quality, homestyle breakfast and lunches made from seasonal, local ingredients. The café, with table service, is a convivial space with rustic tables filled by local families. The takeaway shop next door has counter service and a few dine-in tables (Mon-Fri 8:00-16:00, Sat-Sun from 9:00, 15 Blackfriars Street, tel. 0131/556-6922).

$ Mimi's Bakehouse Picnic Parlour, a handy Royal Mile outpost of a prizewinning bakery, serves up baked goods—try the scones—and sandwiches in their cute and modern shop (daily 9:00-18:00, 250 Canongate, tel. 0131/556-6632).

$ Clarinda's Tea Room, near the bottom of the Royal Mile, is a charming and girlish time warp—a fine and tasty place to relax after touring the Mile or the Palace of Holyroodhouse. Stop in for a quiche, salad, or soup lunch. It's also great for sandwiches and tea and cake anytime (Mon-Sat 9:00-16:30, Sun from 10:00, 69 Canongate, tel. 0131/557-1888).

$$ Hendersons is a bright and casual local chain with good vegetarian dishes to go or eat in (daily 9:00-17:00, 67 Holyrood Road—three minutes off Royal Mile near Scottish Parliament end, tel. 0131/557-1606; for more details, see the Hendersons listing later, under "The New Town").

Historic Pubs Along the Mile

To drink a pint or grab some forgettable pub grub in historic surroundings, consider one of the landmark pubs described on my self-guided walk: **$$ Deacon Brodie's Tavern,** at a dead-center location on the Royal Mile (a sloppy pub on the ground floor with a sloppy restaurant upstairs) or **$$ The World's End Pub,** farther down the Mile at Canongate (a colorful old place dishing up hearty meals from a creative menu in a fun, dark, and noisy space, 4 High Street). Both serve pub meals and are open long hours daily.

THE NEW TOWN

In the Georgian part of town, you'll find a bustling world of office workers, students, and pensioners doing their thing. All of these eateries are within a few minutes' walk of the TI and Waverley Station.

Elegant Spaces near Princes Street

These places provide a staid glimpse at grand old Edinburgh. The ambience is generally better than the food.

Café Royal is a movie producer's dream pub—the perfect *fin de siècle* setting for a coffee, beer, or light meal. (In fact, parts of *Chariots of Fire* were filmed here.) Drop in, if only to admire the 1880 tiles featuring famous inventors (daily 12:00-14:30 & 17:00-21:30, bar food available all day, two blocks from Waverley Mall on 19 West Register Street, tel. 0131/556-1884, www.caferoyaledinburgh.co.uk). There are two eateries here: the noisy **$$ pub** and the dressier **$$$ restaurant,** specializing in oysters, fish, and game (reserve for dinner—it's quite small and understandably popular).

$$$$ The Dome Restaurant, in what was a fancy bank, serves modern international cuisine around a classy bar and under the elegant 19th-century skylight dome. With soft jazz and chic, white-tablecloth ambience, it feels a world apart. Come here not for the food, but for the opulent atmosphere (daily 12:00-23:00, food served until 21:30, reserve for dinner, open for a drink any time under the dome; the adjacent, more intimate Club Room serves food Mon-Thu 10:00-16:00, Fri-Sat until 21:30, closed Sun; 14 George Street, tel. 0131/624-8624, www.thedomeedinburgh.com).

Casual and Cheap near St. Andrew Square

$$ Dishoom, in the New Town, is the first non-London outpost of this popular Bombay café. You'll enjoy upscale Indian cuisine in a bustling, dark, 1920s dining room on the second floor overlooking St. Andrew Square. You can also order from the same menu in the basement bar at night (daily 9:00-23:00, 3A St. Andrew Square, tel. 0131/202-6406).

$ St. Andrew's and St. George's Church Undercroft Café, in the basement of a fine old church, is the cheapest place in town for lunch. Your tiny bill helps support the Church of Scotland (Mon-Fri lunch only, closed Sat-Sun, at 13 George Street, just off St. Andrew Square, tel. 0131/225-3847).

Supermarkets: Marks & Spencer Food Hall offers an assortment of tasty hot foods, prepared sandwiches, fresh bakery items, a wide selection of wines and beverages, and plastic utensils at the checkout queue. It's just a block from the Scott Monument and the picnic-perfect Princes Street Gardens (Mon-Sat 8:00-19:00, Thu until 20:00, Sun 11:00-18:00, Princes Street 54—separate stairway next to main M&S entrance leads directly to food hall, tel. 0131/225-2301). **Sainsbury's** supermarket, a block off Princes Street, also offers grab-and-go items (daily 7:00-22:00, on corner of Rose Street on St. Andrew Square, across the street from Jenners).

Hip Eateries on and near Thistle Street

For something a little more modern and food-focused, head a few more minutes deeper into the New Town to find Thistle Street. This strip and its surrounding lanes are packed with more enticing eateries than the rest of the New Town put together. Browse the options here, but tune into these favorites.

$$$ Le Café St. Honoré, tucked away like a secret bit of old Paris, is a charming place with friendly service and walls lined with wine bottles. It serves French-Scottish cuisine in tight, Old World, cut-glass elegance to a dressy crowd (three-course lunch and dinner specials, daily 12:00-14:00 & 17:30-22:00, reservations smart—ask to sit upstairs, down Thistle Street from Hanover Street, 34 Northwest Thistle Street Lane, tel. 0131/226-2211, www.cafesthonore.com).

$$$ The Bon Vivant is woody, youthful, and candlelit, with a rotating menu of French/Scottish dishes, a good cocktail list, and a companion wine shop next door. They have fun tapas plates and heartier dishes, served either in the bar up front or in the restaurant in back (daily 12:00-22:00, 55 Thistle Street, tel. 0131/225-3275, www.bonvivantedinburgh.co.uk).

$$ Hendersons has fed a generation of New Town vegetarians hearty cuisine and salads. Even carnivores love this place for its delectable salads, desserts, and smoothies. Hendersons has two separate eateries: Their main restaurant, facing Hanover Street, is self-service by day but has table service after 17:00. Each evening after 19:00, they have pleasant live music—generally guitar or jazz (Mon-Sat 9:00-22:00, Sun 10:30-16:00, between Queen and George streets at 94 Hanover Street, tel. 0131/225-2131). Just around the corner on Thistle Street, **Hendersons Vegan** has a strictly vegan menu and feels a bit more casual (daily 12:00-21:30, tel. 0131/225-2605).

$ El Cartel is a youthful place serving up good tacos and other Mexican dishes in a cramped, edgy atmosphere. Enjoy a drink at their sister restaurant the Bon Vivant (listed earlier) while waiting for a table to open up (daily 12:00-22:00, 64 Thistle Street, tel. 0131/226-7171).

IN THE B&B NEIGHBORHOOD

Nearly all of these places (except for The Sheep Heid Inn) are within a 10-minute walk of my recommended B&Bs. For locations, see the map on page 99. For a cozy drink after dinner, visit the recommended pubs in the area (see "Nightlife in Edinburgh," earlier).

Pub Grub

$$ The Salisbury Arms Pub, with a nice garden terrace and separate restaurant area, serves upscale, pleasing traditional classics with yuppie flair in a space that exudes more Martha Stewart and Pottery Barn than traditional public house (book ahead for restaurant, food served daily 12:00-22:00, across from the pool at 58 Dalkeith Road, tel. 0131/667-4518, www. thesalisburyarmsedinburgh.co.uk).

$$ The Old Bell Inn, with an old-time sports-bar ambience— fishing, golf, horses, televisions—serves pub meals. This is a classic "snug pub"—all dark woods and brass beer taps, littered with evocative knickknacks. It comes with sidewalk seating and a mixed-age crowd (bar tables can be reserved, food served daily until 21:15, 233 Causewayside, tel. 0131/668-1573, http://oldbelledinburgh.co.uk).

Other Eateries

$$$$ Aizle is a delicious night out. They serve a set £45 five-course tasting menu based on what's in season—ingredients are listed on the chalkboard (with notice, they can accommodate dietary restrictions). The restaurant is intimate but unpretentious, and they only serve 36 people a night to keep the experience special and unrushed (dinner-only Wed-Sun, this is not a walk-in type of place—book at least a week ahead, 107 St. Leonard's Street—five minutes past the Royal Commonwealth Pool, tel. 0131/662-9349, www.aizle. co.uk).

$$ Southpour is a nice place for a local beer, craft cocktail, or a reliable meal from a menu of salads, sandwiches, meat dishes, and other comfort foods. The brick walls, wood beams, and giant windows give it a warm and open vibe (daily 10:00-22:00, 1 Newington Road, tel. 0131/650-1100).

$$ Ristorante Isola is a calm and casual place with 15 tables surrounding a bright yellow bar. They serve pizzas, pastas, and meat or seafood *secondi* with an emphasis on Sardinian specialties (Mon-Tue 17:00-22:30, Wed-Sun 12:00-22:30, 85 Newington Road, tel. 0131/662-9977).

$$ Voujon Restaurant serves a fusion menu of Bengali and Indian cuisines. Vegetarians appreciate the expansive yet inexpensive offerings (daily 17:00-23:00, 107 Newington Road, tel. 0131/667-5046).

$$ Apiary has an inviting, casual interior and a hit-or-miss, eclectic menu that mingles various international flavors (daily 10:00-15:00 & 17:30-21:00, 33 Newington Road, tel. 0131/668-4999).

Fast Eats

At **$ Edinburgh Bakehouse,** award-winning baker James Lynch makes £1-2 fresh breads, sweets, and meat pies from scratch in this laid-back, nondescript shop. Locals line up for his morning rolls—which earned him the title "baker of the year." Stop by to see the friendly staff and open kitchen in action and judge for yourself (cash only, daily 7:00-16:00 or whenever the goods sell out, open 24 hours from Fri until Sun afternoon to cater to the weekend pub crowd, 101 Newington Road).

$ Earthy is an organic, farm-fresh café and grocery store with a proudly granola attitude. Order from the counter, with its appealing display of freshly prepared salads, sandwiches, and baked goods. Sit in the industrial-mod interior, with rustic picnic benches, or out in the ragtag back garden. In the well-stocked store, assemble a pricey but top-quality picnic (café daily 9:00-17:00, store open until 19:00, 33 Ratcliffe Terrace, tel. 0131/667-2967).

Groceries: Several grocery stores are on the main streets near the restaurants, including Sainsbury's Local and Co-op on South Clerk Road, and Tesco Express and another Sainsbury's Local one block over on Causewayside (all open late—until at least 22:00). Cameron Toll Shopping Centre, about a half-mile south on your way out of town, houses a Sainsbury's superstore for more substantial supplies and gasoline.

Memorable Meals Farther Out

$$$$ Rhubarb Restaurant specializes in Old World elegance. It's in "Edinburgh's most handsome house"—an over-the-top riot of antiques, velvet, tassels, and fringes. The plush dark-rhubarb color theme reminds visitors that this was the place where rhubarb was first grown in Britain. It's a 10-minute walk past the other recommended eateries behind Arthur's Seat, in a huge estate with big, shaggy Highland cattle enjoying their salads al fresco. At night, it's a candlelit wonder. Most spend a wad here. Reserve in advance and dress up if you can (two-course lunch and three-course dinner, daily 12:00-14:00 & 18:00-22:00, afternoon tea served daily 12:00-19:00, in Prestonfield House, Priestfield Road, tel. 0131/662-2303, www.prestonfield.com). For details on their schmaltzy Scottish folk evening, see "Nightlife in Edinburgh," earlier.

$$ The Sheep Heid Inn, Edinburgh's oldest and most inviting public house, is equally notable for its history, date-night appeal, and hearty portions of affordable, classy dishes. It's either a short cab ride or pleasant 30-minute walk from the B&B neighborhood (see page 99), but it's worth the effort to dine in this dreamy setting in the presence of past queens and kings—choose between the bar downstairs, dining room upstairs, or outside in the classic garden courtyard (food served Mon-Fri 12:00-21:00, Sat-Sun 12:00-21:30, 43 The Causeway, tel. 0131/661-7974, www. thesheepheidedinburgh.co.uk).

Edinburgh Connections

BY TRAIN OR BUS

From Edinburgh by Train to: Glasgow (10/hour, 50 minutes), **St. Andrews** (train to Leuchars, 2/hour, 1 hour, then 10-minute bus into St. Andrews), **Stirling** (2/hour, 1 hour), **Pitlochry** (6/day direct, 2 hours), **Inverness** (6/day direct, 3.5 hours, more with transfer), **Oban** (5/day, 4.5 hours, change in Glasgow), **York** (3/hour, 2.5 hours), **London** (2/hour, 4.5 hours), **Durham** (hourly direct, 2 hours, less frequent in winter), **Newcastle** (3/hour, 1.5 hours), **Keswick/Lake District** (8/day to Penrith—more via Carlisle, 2 hours, then 40-minute bus ride to Keswick), **Birmingham** (hourly, 5 hours, less with transfer), **Crewe** (every 2 hours, 3 hours), **Bristol,** near Bath (hourly, 6.5 hours), **Blackpool** (2/hour, 3.5 hours, transfer in Preston). Train info: Tel. 0345-748-4950, www.nationalrail. co.uk.

By Bus: Edinburgh's bus station is in the New Town, just off St. Andrew Square, two blocks north of the train station. Direct buses go to **Glasgow** (Citylink bus #900, 4/hour, 1.5 hours), **Inverness** (express #G90, 2/day, 3.5 hours; slower #M90, 6/day, 4 hours), **Pitlochry** (Citylink #M90, 3/day, 2.5 hours), **Stirling** (every 2 hours on Citylink #909, 1 hour). To reach other destinations in the Highlands—including **Oban, Fort William, Glencoe,** or **Portree** on the Isle of Skye—you'll have to transfer. It's usually fastest to take the train to Glasgow and change to a bus there. For bus info, stop by the station or call Scottish Citylink (tel. 0871-266-3333, www.citylink.co.uk). Additional long-distance routes may be operated by National Express (www.nationalexpress. com) or Megabus (www.megabus.com).

BY PLANE

Edinburgh Airport is located eight miles northwest of the center (airport code: EDI, tel. 0844-481-8989, www.edinburghairport. com). **Taxis** or **Uber rides** between the airport and city center are about £20-25 (25 minutes to downtown or Dalkeith Road). The airport is also well connected to central Edinburgh by tram and bus. Just follow signs outside; the tram tracks are straight ahead, and the bus stop is to the right, along the main road in front of the terminal. **Trams** make several stops in town, including along Princes Street and at St. Andrew Square (£5.50, buy ticket from machine, runs every 10 minutes from early morning until 23:30, 35 minutes, www.edinburghtrams.com).

The Lothian **Airlink bus #100** drops you at Waverley Bridge (£4.50, £7.50 round-trip, runs every 10 minutes, 30 minutes, tel. 0131/555-6363, http://lothianbuses.co.uk). Whether you take the tram or bus to the center, to continue on to my recommended

B&Bs south of the city center, you can either take a taxi (about £7) or hop on a city bus (for directions, see "Sleeping in Edinburgh," earlier). To get from the B&Bs *to* the Airlink or tram stops downtown, you can take a taxi...or ride a city bus to North Bridge, turn left at the grand Balmoral Hotel, and walk a short distance down Princes Street. Turn right up St. Andrew Street to catch the tram at St. Andrew Square, or continue up to the next bridge, Waverley, for the Airlink bus.

ROUTE TIPS FOR DRIVERS HEADING SOUTH

It's 100 miles south from Edinburgh to Hadrian's Wall; to Durham, it's another 50 miles.

To Hadrian's Wall: From Edinburgh, Dalkeith Road leads south and eventually becomes the A-68 (handy Cameron Toll supermarket with cheap gas is on the left as you leave Edinburgh Town, 10 minutes south of Edinburgh; gas and parking behind store). The A-68 road takes you to Hadrian's Wall in 2.5 hours. You'll pass Jedburgh and its abbey after one hour. (For one last shot of Scotland shopping, there's a coach tour's delight just before Jedburgh, with kilt makers, woolens, and a sheepskin shop.) Across from Jedburgh's lovely abbey is a free parking lot, a good visitors center, and pay toilets. The England/Scotland border is a fun, quick stop (great view, ice cream, and tea caravan). Just after the turn for Colwell, turn right onto the A-6079, and roller-coaster four miles down to Low Brunton. Then turn right onto the B-6318, and stay on it by turning left at Chollerford, following the Roman wall westward.

To Durham: If you're heading straight to Durham, you can take the scenic coastal route on the A-1 (a few more miles than the A-68, but similar time), which takes you near Holy Island and Bamburgh Castle.

PRACTICALITIES

This section covers just the basics on traveling in Scotland (for much more information, see *Rick Steves Scotland*). You'll find free advice on specific topics at www.ricksteves.com/tips.

MONEY

For currency, Scotland uses the pound sterling (£), also called a "quid": 1 pound (£1) = about $1.30. One pound is broken into 100 pence (p). To convert prices in pounds to dollars, add about 30 percent: £20 = about $26, £50 = about $65. (Check www.oanda.com for the latest exchange rates.)

Like England, Scotland issues its own pound notes. Scottish pounds are technically interchangeable across Great Britain but sometimes are not accepted by businesses in England. Banks in Scotland or England can convert your Scottish pounds into English pounds at no charge.

The standard way for travelers to get pounds is to withdraw money from an ATM (which locals call "cashpoints") using a debit card, ideally with a Visa or MasterCard logo. To keep your cash, cards, and valuables safe, wear a money belt.

Before departing, call your bank or credit-card company: Confirm that your card(s) will work overseas, ask about international transaction fees, and alert them that you'll be making withdrawals in Europe. Also ask for the PIN number for your credit card—you may need it for Europe's "chip-and-PIN" payment machines (see below; allow time for your bank to mail your PIN to you).

Dealing with "Chip and PIN": Most credit and debit cards now have chips that authenticate and secure transactions. European cardholders insert their chip card into the payment slot, then enter a PIN. (Until recently, most US cards required a signature.) Any American card with a chip will work at Europe's hotels, restaurants, and shops—although sometimes the clerk may ask for a signature. But some self-service payment machines—such as those at train stations, toll roads, or unattended gas pumps—may not accept your card, even if you know the PIN. If your card won't work, look for a cashier who can process the transaction manually—or pay in cash.

Dynamic Currency Conversion: If merchants or hoteliers offer to convert your purchase price into dollars (called dynamic currency conversion, or DCC), refuse this "service." You'll pay more in fees for the expensive convenience of seeing your charge in dollars. If an ATM offers to "lock in" or "guarantee" your conversion rate, choose "proceed without conversion." Other prompts might state, "You can be charged in dollars: Press YES for dollars, NO for pounds." Always choose the local currency.

STAYING CONNECTED

The simplest solution is to bring your own device—mobile phone, tablet, or laptop—and use it just as you would at home (following the tips below, such as connecting to free Wi-Fi whenever possible). The following instructions apply in Scotland and across Great Britain.

To call Great Britain from a US or Canadian number: Whether you're phoning from a landline, your own mobile phone, or a Skype account, you're making an international call. Dial 011-44 and then the area code (minus its initial zero) and local number. (The 011 is our international access code, and 44 is Great Britain's country code.) If dialing from a mobile phone, you can enter + in place of the international access code—press and hold the 0 key.

To call Great Britain from a European country: Dial 00-44 followed by the area code (minus its initial zero) and local number. (The 00 is Europe's international access code.)

To call within Great Britain: If you're dialing within an area code, just dial the local number; but if you're calling outside your area code, you have to dial both the area code (which starts with a 0) and the local number.

To call from Great Britain to another country: Dial 00 followed by the country code (for example, 1 for the US or Canada), then the area code and number. If you're calling European countries whose phone numbers begin with 0, you'll usually have to omit that 0 when you dial.

Tips: If you bring your own mobile phone, consider getting an international plan; most providers offer a global calling plan that cuts the per-minute cost of phone calls and texts, and a flat-fee data plan.

Use Wi-Fi whenever possible. Most hotels and many cafés offer free Wi-Fi, and you'll likely also find it at tourist informa-

Sleep Code

Hotels are classified based on the average price of a typical en suite double room with breakfast in high season.

$$$$	**Splurge:** Most rooms over £160
$$$	**Pricier:** £120-160
$$	**Moderate:** £80-120
$	**Budget:** £40-80
¢	**Backpacker:** Under £40
RS%	**Rick Steves discount**

Unless otherwise noted, credit cards are accepted and free Wi-Fi is available. Comparison-shop by checking prices at several hotels (on each hotel's own website, on a booking site, or by email). For the best deal, *always book directly with the hotel*. Ask for a discount if paying in cash; if the listing includes **RS%**, request a Rick Steves discount.

tion offices (TIs), major museums, and public-transit hubs. With Wi-Fi you can use your phone or tablet to make free or inexpensive domestic and international calls via a calling app such as Skype, FaceTime, or Google+ Hangouts. When you can't find Wi-Fi, you can use your cellular network to connect to the Internet, send texts, or make voice calls. When you're done, avoid further charges by manually switching off "data roaming" or "cellular data."

It's possible to stay connected without a mobile device. You can make calls from your hotel (or the rare public phone), and get online using public computers (there's usually one in your hotel lobby). Most hotels charge a high fee for international calls—ask for rates before you dial. For more on phoning, see www.ricksteves. com/phoning. For a one-hour talk on "Traveling with a Mobile Device," see www.ricksteves.com/travel-talks.

SLEEPING

I've categorized my recommended accommodations based on price, indicated with a dollar-sign rating (see sidebar). I recommend reserving rooms in advance, particularly during peak season. Once your dates are set, check the specific price for your preferred stay at several hotels. You can do this either by comparing prices on sites such as Hotels.com or Booking.com, or by checking the hotels' own websites. To get the best deal, contact my family-run hotels directly by phone or email. When you go direct, the owner avoids any third-party commission, giving them wiggle room to offer you a discount, a nicer room, or free breakfast. If you prefer to book online or are considering a hotel chain, it's to your advantage to use the hotel's website.

For complicated requests, send an email with the following information: number and type of rooms; number of nights; arrival date; departure date; and any special requests. Use the European style for writing dates: day/month/year. Hoteliers typically ask for your credit-card number as a deposit. In general, hotel prices can soften if you do any of the following: offer to pay cash, stay at least three nights, or travel off-season.

Know the terminology: An "en suite" room has a bathroom (toilet and shower/tub) actually inside the room; a room with a "private bathroom" can mean that the bathroom is all yours, but it's across the hall. If you want your own bathroom inside the room, request "en suite."

Compared to hotels, B&Bs and guesthouses give you double the cultural intimacy for half the price. Many B&Bs take credit cards, but may add the card service fee to your bill (about 3 percent). If you do need to pay cash for your room, plan ahead to have enough on hand when you check out.

EATING

I've categorized my recommended eateries based on price, indicated with a dollar-sign rating (see sidebar).

The traditional fry-up or full Scottish breakfast, which is usually included at your B&B or hotel, comes with your choice of eggs, Canadian-style bacon and/or sausage, a grilled tomato, sautéed mushrooms, baked beans, and often haggis, black pudding, or a dense potato scone. If it's too much for you, only order the items you want.

To dine affordably at classier restaurants, look for "early-bird specials" (offered about 17:30–19:00, last order by 19:00, sometimes on weekdays only). Smart travelers use pubs (short for "public houses") to eat, drink, and make new friends. Pub grub is Scotland's best eating value. For about $15–20, you'll get a basic hot lunch or dinner. The menu is hearty and traditional: stews, soups, fish-and-chips, meat, cabbage, and potatoes, plus often a few Italian or Indian-style dishes. Meals are usually served from 12:00 to 14:00 and from 18:00 to 20:00, not throughout the day. Order drinks and meals at the bar; they might bring it to you when it's ready, or you'll pick it up at the bar. Pay as you order, and don't tip unless there's full table service.

Most pubs have lagers (cold, refreshing, American-style beer), ales (amber-colored, cellar-temperature beer), bitters (hop-flavored ale, perhaps the most typical British beer), and stouts (dark and somewhat bitter, like Guinness).

While bar-hopping tourists generally think in terms of beer, many Scottish pubs are just as enthusiastic about serving whisky. If you are unfamiliar with whisky (what Americans call "Scotch" and the Irish call "whiskey"), it's a great conversation starter. Pubs often have dozens of whiskies available.

Restaurant Price Code

I've assigned each eatery a price category, based on the average cost of a typical main course. Drinks, desserts, and splurge items (steak and seafood) can raise the price considerably.

$$$$ **Splurge:** Most main courses over £20
$$$ **Pricier:** £15-20
$$ **Moderate:** £10-15
$ **Budget:** Under £10

In Scotland, carryout fish-and-chips and other takeout food is $; a basic pub or sit-down eatery is $$; a gastropub or casual but more upscale restaurant is $$$; and a swanky splurge is $$$$.

Tipping: If a service charge is included in the bill, it's not necessary to tip. Otherwise, it's appropriate to tip about 10-12 percent for good service.

TRANSPORTATION

By Train: Great Britain's 100-mph train system is one of Europe's best...and most expensive. To see if a rail pass could save you money—as it often does in Britain—check www.ricksteves.com/rail. If you're buying point-to-point tickets, you'll get the best deals if you book in advance, leave after rush hour (after 9:30), or ride the bus. Train reservations are free and recommended for long journeys or any trip on Sundays (reserve at any train station or online). For train schedules, see www.nationalrail.co.uk or Germany's excellent all-Europe website, www.bahn.com.

By Car: A car is useful for scouring the remote rural sights, but it's an expensive headache in big cities. It's cheaper to arrange most car rentals from the US. For tips on your insurance options, see www.ricksteves.com/cdw, and for route planning, consult www.viamichelin.com. Bring your driver's license. Speedy motorways (comparable to our freeways) let you cover long distances in a snap. Remember that the Scottish drive on the left side of the road (and the driver sits on the right side of the car). You'll quickly master Scotland's many roundabouts: Traffic moves clockwise, cars inside the roundabout have the right-of-way, and entering traffic yields (look to your right as you merge). Note that "camera cops" strictly enforce speed limits by automatically snapping photos of speeders' license plates, then mailing them a ticket.

Local road etiquette is similar to that in the US. Ask your car-rental company about the rules of the road, read the UK Department for Transport's *Highway Code* (www.gov.uk/highway-code), or check the US State Department website (www.

travel.state.gov, select "International Travel," then "Country Information," then search for your destination and click "Travel and Transportation").

By Bus: Most long-haul domestic routes in Scotland are operated by Scottish Citylink (www.citylink.co.uk). Longer-distance routes (especially those to England) are operated by National Express (www.nationalexpress.com) or Megabus (www.megabus.com).

HELPFUL HINTS

Emergency Help: To summon the **police** or an **ambulance**, call 999 or 112. For passport problems, call the **US Consulate in Edinburgh** (tel. 0131/556-8315, https://uk.usembassy.gov/embassy-consulates/edinburgh) or the Canadian Consulate in Edinburgh (mobile 0770-235-9916, www.unitedkingdom.gc.ca).

Theft or Loss: To replace a passport, you'll need to go in person to an embassy or consulate (see above). Cancel and replace your credit and debit cards by calling these 24-hour US numbers collect: Visa: tel. 303/967-1096, MasterCard: tel. 636/722-7111, American Express: tel. 336/393-1111. In Britain, to make a collect call to the US, dial 0-800-89-0011; press zero or stay on the line for an operator. File a police report either on the spot or within a day or two; you'll need it to submit an insurance claim for lost or stolen rail passes or travel gear, and it can help with replacing your passport or credit and debit cards. For more information, see www.ricksteves.com/help.

Time: Scotland uses the 24-hour clock. It's the same through 12:00 noon, then keep going: 13:00, 14:00, and so on. Scotland, like the rest of Great Britain, is five/eight hours ahead of the East/West Coasts of the US (and one hour earlier than most of continental Europe).

Holidays and Festivals: Great Britain celebrates many holidays, which can close sights and attract crowds (book hotel rooms ahead). For information on holidays and festivals, check Scotland's tourism website: www.visitscotland.com. For a simple list showing major—though not all—events, see www.ricksteves.com/festivals.

Numbers and Stumblers: What Americans call the second floor of a building is the first floor in Europe. Europeans write dates as day/month/year, so Christmas 2020 is 25/12/20. For most measurements, Great Britain uses the metric system: A kilogram is 2.2 pounds, and a liter is about a quart. For driving distances, they use miles.

PRACTICALITIES

RESOURCES FROM RICK STEVES

This Snapshot guide is excerpted from my latest edition of *Rick Steves Scotland*, one of many titles in my ever-expanding series of guidebooks on European travel. I also produce a public television series, *Rick Steves' Europe*, and a public radio show, *Travel with Rick Steves*. My website, www.ricksteves.com, offers free travel information, a forum for travelers' comments, guidebook updates, my travel blog, an online travel store, and information on European rail passes and our tours of Europe. If you're bringing a mobile device on your trip, you can download my free Rick Steves Audio Europe app, featuring podcasts of my radio shows, my Edinburgh Royal Mile Walk audio tour, and travel interviews about Scotland. You can get Rick Steves Audio Europe via Apple's App Store, Google Play, or the Amazon Appstore. For more information, see www.ricksteves.com/audioeurope.

ADDITIONAL RESOURCES

Tourist Information: www.visitscotland.com
Passports and Red Tape: www.travel.state.gov
Packing List: www.ricksteves.com/packing
Travel Insurance: www.ricksteves.com/insurance
Cheap Flights: www.kayak.com or www.google.com/flights
Airplane Carry-on Restrictions: www.tsa.gov
Updates for This Book: www.ricksteves.com/update

HOW WAS YOUR TRIP?

To share your tips, concerns, and discoveries after using this book, please fill out the survey at www.ricksteves.com/feedback. Thanks in advance—it helps a lot.

INDEX

INDEX

INDEX

Explore Europe

At ricksteves.com you can browse through thousands of articles, videos, photos and radio interviews, plus find a wealth of money-saving travel tips for planning your dream trip. And with our mobile-friendly website, you can easily access all this great travel information anywhere you go.

TV Shows

Preview the places you'll visit by watching entire half-hour episodes of Rick Steves' Europe (choose from all 100 shows) on-demand, for free.

your travel dreams into affordable reality

Radio Interviews

Enjoy ready access to Rick's vast library of radio interviews covering travel

tips and cultural insights that relate specifically to your Europe travel plans.

Travel Forums

Learn, ask, share! Our online community of savvy travelers is a great resource

for first-time travelers to Europe, as well as seasoned pros. You'll find forums on each country, plus travel tips and restaurant/hotel reviews. You can even ask one of our well-traveled staff to chime in with an opinion.

Travel News

Subscribe to our free Travel News e-newsletter, and get monthly updates from Rick on what's happening in Europe.

Rick's Free Travel App

AUDIO EUROPE

Get your FREE **Rick Steves Audio Europe**™ app to enjoy…

- Dozens of self-guided tours of Europe's top museums, sights and historic walks
- Hundreds of tracks filled with cultural insights and sightseeing tips from Rick's radio interviews
- All organized into handy geographic playlists
- For Apple and Android

With Rick whispering in your ear, Europe gets even better.

Find out more at ricksteves.com

Gear up for your next adventure at ricksteves.com

Light Luggage

Pack light and right with Rick Steves' affordable, custom-designed rolling carry-on bags, backpacks, day packs and shoulder bags.

Accessories

From packing cubes to moneybelts and beyond, Rick has personally selected the travel goodies that will help your trip go smoother.

Experience maximum Europe

Save time and energy

This guidebook is your independent-travel toolkit. But for all it delivers, it's still up to you to devote the time and energy it takes to manage the preparation and logistics that are essential for a happy trip. If that's a hassle, there's a solution.

Rick Steves Tours

A Rick Steves tour takes you to Europe's most interesting places with great

with minimum stress

guides and small groups of 28 or less. We follow Rick's favorite itineraries, ride in comfy buses, stay in family-run hotels, and bring you intimately close to the Europe you've traveled so far to see. Most importantly, we take away the logistical headaches so you can focus on the fun.

travelers—nearly half of them repeat customers— along with us on four dozen different itineraries, from Ireland to Italy to Athens. Is a Rick Steves tour the right fit for your travel dreams? Find out at rick steves.com, where you can also request Rick's latest tour catalog. Europe is best experienced with happy travel partners. We hope you can join us.

Join the fun

This year we'll take thousands of free-spirited

BEST OF GUIDES

Full color easy-to-scan format, focusing on Europe's most popular destinations and sights.

Best of England
Best of Europe
Best of France
Best of Germany
Best of Ireland
Best of Italy
Best of Spain

COMPREHENSIVE GUIDES

City, country, and regional guides with detailed coverage for a multi-week trip exploring the most iconic sights and venturing off the beaten track.

Amsterdam & the Netherlands
Barcelona
Belgium: Bruges, Brussels,
  Antwerp & Ghent
Berlin
Budapest
Croatia & Slovenia
Eastern Europe
England
Florence & Tuscany
France
Germany
Great Britain
Greece: Athens & the Peloponnese
Iceland
Ireland
Istanbul
Italy
London
Paris
Portugal
Prague & the Czech Republic
Provence & the French Riviera
Rome
Scandinavia
Scotland
Spain
Switzerland
Venice
Vienna, Salzburg & Tirol

HE BEST OF ROME

ne, Italy's capital, is studded with
nan remnants and floodlit-fountain
res. From the Vatican to the Colos-
n, with crazy traffic in between, Rome
nderful, huge, and exhausting. The
ds, the heat, and the weighty history

of the Eternal City where Caesars walked
can make tourists wilt. Recharge by taking siestas, gelato breaks, and after-dark
walks, strolling from one atmospheric
square to another in the refreshing evening air.

*d Pantheon—which
est dome until the
ly 2,000 years old
y over 1,500).*

*of Athens in the Vat-
fies the humanistic
ce.*

*gladiators fought
nother, entertaining*

*> Rome ristorante.
ds at St. Peter's
seriously.*

Rick Steves guidebooks are published by Avalon Travel,
an imprint of Perseus Books, a Hachette Book Group company.

POCKET GUIDES

Compact, full color city guides with the essentials for shorter trips.

Amsterdam	Paris
Athens	Prague
Barcelona	Rome
Florence	Venice
Italy's Cinque Terre	Vienna
London	
Munich & Salzburg	

SNAPSHOT GUIDES

Focused single-destination coverage.

Basque Country: Spain & France
Copenhagen & the Best of Denmark
Dublin
Dubrovnik
Edinburgh
Hill Towns of Central Italy
Krakow, Warsaw & Gdansk
Lisbon
Loire Valley
Madrid & Toledo
Milan & the Italian Lakes District
Naples & the Amalfi Coast
Normandy
Northern Ireland
Norway
Reykjavík
Sevilla, Granada & Southern Spain
St. Petersburg, Helsinki & Tallinn
Stockholm

CRUISE PORTS GUIDES

Reference for cruise ports of call.

Mediterranean Cruise Ports
Scandinavian & Northern European
Cruise Ports

Complete your library with...

TRAVEL SKILLS & CULTURE

Study up on travel skills and gain insight on history and culture.

Europe 101
Europe Through the Back Door
European Christmas
European Easter
European Festivals
Postcards from Europe
Travel as a Political Act

PHRASE BOOKS & DICTIONARIES

French
French, Italian & German
German
Italian
Portuguese
Spanish

PLANNING MAPS

Britain, Ireland & London
Europe
France & Paris
Germany, Austria & Switzerland
Ireland
Italy
Spain & Portugal

Rick Steves books are available from your favorite bookseller.
Many guides are available as ebooks.

Avalon Travel
Hachette Book Group
1700 Fourth Street
Berkeley, CA 94710

Text © 2018 by Rick Steves' Europe, Inc. All rights reserved.
Maps © 2018 by Rick Steves' Europe, Inc. All rights reserved.

Printed in Canada by Friesens.
Second Edition. First printing May 2018.

ISBN 978-1-63121-820-0

For the latest on Rick's lectures, guidebooks, tours, public television series, and public
radio show, contact Rick Steves' Europe, 130 Fourth Avenue North, Edmonds, WA 98020,
425/771-8303, www.ricksteves.com, rick@ricksteves.com.

Rick Steves' Europe
Managing Editor: Jennifer Madison Davis
Special Publications Manager: Risa Laib
Assistant Managing Editor: Cathy Lu
Editors: Glenn Eriksen, Julie Fanselow, Tom Griffin, Katherine Gustafson, Mary Keils,
    Suzanne Kotz, Rosie Leutzinger, Carrie Shepherd
Editorial & Production Assistant: Jessica Shaw
Editorial Intern: Kevin Teeter
Researcher: Cathy Lu
Contributor: Gene Openshaw
Graphic Content Director: Sandra Hundacker
Maps & Graphics: David C. Hoerlein, Lauren Mills, Mary Rostad

Avalon Travel
Senior Editor and Series Manager: Maddy McPrasher
Editor: Jamie Andrade
Editor: Sierra Machado
Copy Editor: Maggie Ryan
Proofreaders: Kelly Lydick, Patrick Collins
Indexer: Stephen Callahan
Production & Typesetting: Christine DeLorenzo, Kit Anderson, Lisi Baldwin, Rue
    Flaherty, Jane Musser, Sarah Wildfang
Cover Design: Kimberly Glyder Design
Maps & Graphics: Kat Bennett, Lohnes & Wright

Front Cover: Victoria Street © Madrabothair | Dreamstime.com
Title Page: © Dominic Arizona Bonuccelli
Additional Photography: Dominic Arizona Bonuccelli, Rich Earl, Jennifer Hauseman,
Cameron Hewitt, David C. Hoerlein, Lauren Mills, Rhonda Pelikan, Jennifer Schutte,
Rick Steves, Gretchen Strauch, Wikimedia Commons(PD-Art/PD-US), © Stephen
C. Dickson cc BY-SA 4.0. Photos are used by permission and are the property of the
original copyright owners.

Let's on

to end.

Follow Rick on
social media!